Doing the M&A Deal: A Quick Access Field Manual and Guide
Second Edition

Second Edition

Michael P. Gendron

TABLE OF CONTENTS

Preface

This field manual and guide will take the business leader and his team of experts through the Mergers & Acquisitions operations process from Due Diligence to completed integration or transition. Many books are sold that describe how to value acquisitions, and how to negotiate a fair price. This book describes the entire systematic process to fully execute the transaction. Throughout the text, action steps are highlighted using underlined italic text to simplify the guide's use. The numbering convention used, for example "2.3.2 – Executive Advocates" could be used as a basis for work paper or filing convention.

This manual outlines the timing, a description of the personnel requirements, and actual activities necessary to complete a successful merger. The manual provides example analyses and forms to serve as a guideline to the M&A teams, but since each transaction varies, they are merely templates to consider rather than requirements. As you proceed through a transaction, the keys to success will be:
Management experience and judgment to focus on those critical items that will make the transaction a success;
Effective planning and selection of the right team members;
Clear and open communication with all constituents.

Although more than 50% of mergers fail to meet investment objectives, those organizations that carefully manage the transition process reap exceptional rewards.

INTRODUCTION

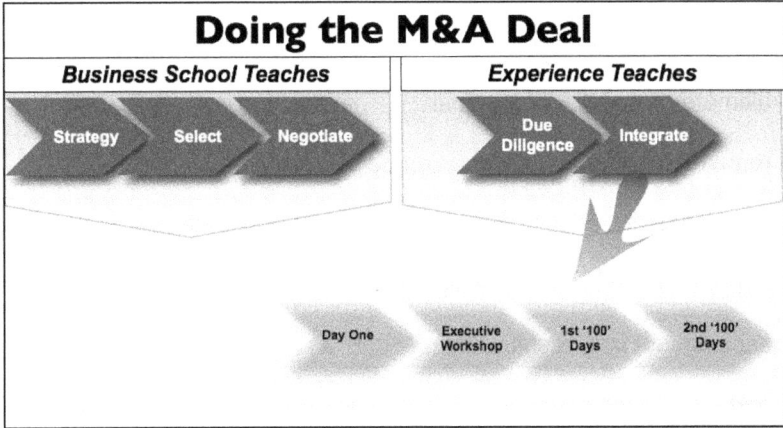

Doing the M&A Deal

Business School Teaches	Experience Teaches
Strategy · Select · Negotiate	Due Diligence · Integrate
	Day One · Executive Workshop · 1st '100' Days · 2nd '100' Days

This Field Manual will discuss the _experience side of Doing the M&A Deal and will not describe strategy, target selection process or valuation techniques_. This Manual outlines the steps required to successfully complete any Merger & Acquisition (M&A) transaction. The guide will define practical, proven methods:

o   To thoroughly examine the acquisition candidates during Due Diligence review,

o   To provide the basis for financial experts to value a target, and

o   To identify the critical steps necessary to realize the value through effective integration management.

The manual is prepared as a transaction actually occurs from Due Diligence, through Day One after closing, to the First and Second 100 Days after acquisition. As each phase is completed, the ultimate probability of the deal's success increases. The manual requires that the entire operation be assessed - all functions, companies, locations, and constituents - to avoid missing opportunity. Based on the significance of a particular area, the assessment may result with no action, since resources are limited and the Company should prioritize activities based on risks and benefits. Ideally, the M&A executive team will remain consistent throughout the transaction, and will execute the program from Due Diligence through Integration. In the planning stage, the M&A executive will present the findings, goals and objectives, timelines, estimated costs, benefits, and contingency plans reflected in the M&A Deal Valuation. In addition, each executive will personally review his/her functional area with the M&A team to ensure proper alignment among the functions and to ensure a common understanding of the transaction.

M&A is a high-risk activity - more than 50% of acquisitions fail to reach established objectives.

This manual presents master matrices and checklists, and refers to traditional project management techniques to obtain the expected benefits. The extent or depth of work depends upon the risk-taking assumptions made by Company leadership - - less work equals more risk assumed. Executive judgment, however, is an essential part of an effective integration. The overall structure of this Pocket Guide follows the life of the transaction:

PRE-DEAL:

o   Complete the Due Diligence to provide the basis of a proper valuation, a summary of upsides and downsides, and a foundation for integration planning.

o   Define a "To Be" or future state for the combined companies at specific periods. For example, some integration projects may require years before the ultimate *"To Be"* state is completed. Such long-term projects should have intermediate goals to measure progress - i.e. year 1, year 2.

o   Prepare the high-level preliminary integration plan that reflects the basic investment decisions required to reach the *"To Be"* state. Executives must agree to a high-level model, and the preliminary integration planning required before detailed planning begins.

PRE-DEAL/DEAL:

o Complete an <u>integration-planning</u> meeting to review the issues, possible solutions, and identify additional investments and action plans required to reach the future state. The M&A executive leader should obtain executive team consensus.

POST DEAL:

o <u>Execute Day-One activities</u> that are essential to establish governance, financial control, communications, and retain the critical value items (e.g. key employees, vendors, and customers, intellectual property...) acquired.

o During the First 100 Days <u>confirm preliminary assumptions, finalize the detailed analysis and strategy, finish the detailed design, and then execute - build and implement processes.</u>

o During the Second 100 days <u>sustain the routine activities, begin to harvest the initial benefits, and reassess the strategy and synergies</u> expected. <u>Define and implement corrective actions.</u>

While the size and complexity of every deal is different, it is important to move quickly when integrating. Increase integration staff size for a larger transaction to accelerate the transformation process and maintain the First 100 Day and Second 100 Day pace. A prolonged transition will increase business risk because more than one organization requires more coordination than a single, unified business unit. Long transitions can be very expensive, both directly and indirectly, as inefficiency during a transition may reach 50%. A prolonged integration will also adversely affect interactions with customers, vendors, and employees due to changing relationships, and implementation of various policies and procedures as the companies combine to a single unit. Note in Exhibit 1 that the cumulative cost curve increases significantly over time, due to inefficiency and business disruption, while the actual acquisition cost remains constant.

Exhibit 1

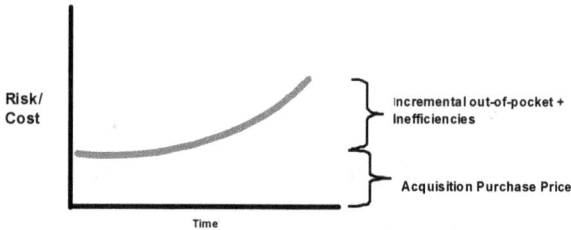

Risk/ Cost

Incremental out-of-pocket + Inefficiencies

Acquisition Purchase Price

Time

Business risks and costs increase exponentially with time - cost may not be limited to your investment, but may include your base business.

Always assign the best personnel to the task - i.e. Due Diligence or Integration - whether they are employees or outsourced staff and executives. Remember, just because you are the acquirer, it does not always mean that you have better processes, better people or better facilities. Without bias, assess the current environment, plan a "To Be" state, and then ruthlessly execute the plan.

The Pocket Guide will explain basic concepts to be applied first at a high level during pre-deal activities, and then much more thoroughly after the deal is completed and the Company has complete access to the Acquired Company resources, records and processes.

18

There are numerous templates included in this field manual. They are designed to help the reader think through a transaction and don't require rigid completion. Judgment is essential as you work through a transaction.

CASE STUDY - THE STRATEGY

The private equity (PE) firm decided to roll-up a group of small regional companies in the medical supplies market segment. Their goal was to execute a series of transactions - perhaps as many as 10-12 small regional companies - to achieve a critical mass of about $100 million annual revenue. They believed that with such a large presence, economies of scale could be achieved in both operating efficiencies as well as purchasing power. Acquisition pricing was targeted at a multiple of about 3-4 x EBITDA. Once the critical mass of about $100 million was reached, the PE firm expected a higher multiple, due to the transaction size. As the Companies were effectively integrated, synergies and economies of scale would contribute to higher earnings. The PE Company did not expect to invest significant amounts, since the individual companies acquired were to be well-managed companies requiring minimal investment.

In the ideal world, some of these companies would have small manufacturing facilities that could produce non-sterile, disposable medical supplies. The roll-up would broaden distribution of the manufactured products through a captive channel, resulting with increased production, higher utilization of facilities and overall improved margins.

Their strategy included establishing regional warehouses to limit local supply distribution to "A" and "B" classification inventory SKU's. "C" classified items - those used least frequently -would be concentrated in a central warehouse for national distribution. They believed that this strategy would substantially reduce national inventory investment, while providing adequate service to their customers.

The regional distributors varying levels of service (ranging from outstanding to merely adequate) concerned the PE executives. However, they believed that with the regional warehouse concept, national service levels could reach above average performance.

For this roll-up to be effective, they needed to move quickly before the 'mom & pop' regional suppliers recognized the Company's goal. Awareness of the roll-up might potentially increase company purchase price. Their plan was to complete the 10+ acquisitions within a 90-day period to avoid such price escalation.

The private equity executives retained several health-care executives on-call for just such an acquisition strategy. They engaged a COO and CFO to manage this particular M&A process, with the support of other PE executives, staff and when necessary, outside technical experts.

Analysts identified a series of potential acquisitions, and initiated the acquisition strategy.

As individual negotiations proceeded, the COO and CFO began the Due Diligence process. Due to the accelerated timing, numerous technical experts were hired to complete narrow functional Due Diligence segments. While these experts were aware of the overall roll-up strategy, timing prohibited them from performing as thorough a review as they considered appropriate. At each site, the Due Diligence priority drifted to, "Identify issues that would cause us not

21

to acquire the company. Do the systems & processes work at the facilities acquired?" As such, review elements that might affect the overall national strategy were sometimes missed.

Although the Company used a master acquisition template describing acceptable risks as the basis for each acquisition, the negotiator was allowed some freedom to modify acquisition terms to finalize the deals on time.

The COO and CFO concentrated all available time on completing the deals, while creating high-level checklists that identified major integration issues. As a standard rule, the PE group bought company assets and avoided assuming liabilities, except accounts payable directly related to the procurement of inventory and production essentials. Accounts receivable and related reserves were acquired, with a true-up scheduled at 90 days.

1 Due Diligence

Assemble the Due Diligence team of experts unique to the deal characteristics. For example, if the transaction is a Manufacturing Acquisition, the team should include Manufacturing Experts. If in-house experts are not available, hire staff from outside the Company, since the Due Diligence review may be the best chance to gain clear insight into all the critical elements of the target business.

Review the target company's operations and business strategy (through examination of documents, processes and discussions with key constituents, such as employees, customers and vendors) to *validate valuation assumptions, to identify upsides and downsides to valuation, and start integration planning.* The Due Diligence reviews are intense, time constrained, and should be focused on critical issues.

Review the purpose of the acquisition with the Due Diligence team to establish the frame of reference for their review. For example, if you acquire a company to obtain patents and other intellectual property, physical assets such as office equipment, buildings, and transportation equipment may have little impact on the deal valuation or execution.

Due Diligence is a review of a target operation to better understand the target and to value the acquisition. Due Diligence goals are to:

- o Validate the valuation assumptions;
- o Identify significant upsides and downsides to the valuation;
- o Identify significant integration or transition issues.

Due Diligence reviews – examine and assess, on a prioritized basis, the following:

- o People, including all constituents;
- o Processes;
- o Plant and all assets used in a company operation;
- o Products & product pipeline;
- o Market, competitors and competitive conditions.

1.1   Purpose of the Acquisition

Define the purpose of the acquisition so that the Due Diligence team understands the acquisition strategy and the critical success factors to the valuation.

Identify the major purpose as one of the following to help determine the critical success factors, which will accelerate corporate value (higher earnings, reduced investment and so forth). Identifying the purpose will help the selection of the Due Diligence team - engaging the experts that will assess the critical elements of value.

PROCESS: Obtain unique or patented processes. Examples include a fully implemented *Lean Manufacturing* process, new product development process, logistics or sale processes.

MARKET EXPANSION: Expand product lines or geographic reach. Examples include acquiring a European presence, adding product line extensions, or entirely new product platforms to the Company portfolio.

PEOPLE/CONSTITUENTS: Acquire people or constituents, or establish linkage to critical organizations or individuals. Examples include adding key employees, suppliers/vendors, or customers.

FINANCIAL: Acquire entities that expand the Company's strategic foundation. Examples include a manufacturing company buying a service company, or a plastics manufacturer buying an engineering company that can dramatically improve profitability.

1.1.1.1 *Identify the key valuation assumptions within the stated strategy.* For example, if R&D personnel are a key to valuation, understand what is necessary to protect that value, define upside/downside risks related to key personnel, and develop transition/integration plans that preserve the value. Prioritize all efforts to preserve those valuation keys. If a patented process is the acquisition strategic goal, validate the patents and related processes, assess as to future value to the company, and establish any integration plans as a priority.

If a target company has multiple locations, evaluate the locations to determine their importance to the valuation. If a location has minimal impact on valuation, the location may not be prioritized or reviewed in detail. For example, a European Engineering/R&D facility may employ very few people and have a small asset investment, but may represent a

26

significant benefit to the transaction. In such a case, a

thorough assessment of that organization will help ensure the

value of the investment. Note in the following example that

Company A's engineers are very small in relation to the total

Company A or Company B employees, but if they represent

the key to value, through their innovative development

practices and creative genius, plans should be developed to

protect this group of employees. Each employee group has

its own priorities, personal characteristics, and formal and

informal work methods. Groups may overlap and also may

have some characteristics in common with others.

Exhibit 2
Two Companies Merge

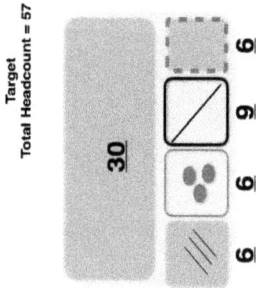

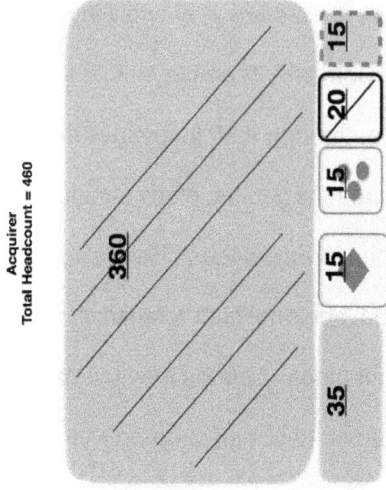

Target
Total Headcount = 57

30

6   6   9   6

Acquirer
Total Headcount = 460

360

35   15   15   20   15

Note: The size of the circle indicates relative # of employees.

= Engineering   = Sales/Marketing   = Finance

= Factory hourly   = Info Tech   = Other Admin

28

Exhibit 2 depicts an R&D company on the left. Note that there are no sales and marketing personnel in Company A, and more than half of the employees are engineers. This company will likely have an entirely different culture than one with nearly 75% of the employees as factory hourly employees.

1.2 Validate Valuation Assumptions

Validate valuation assumptions by understanding and identifying the value drivers: a general sales increase is not a value driver, however launching a new product line is a driver that achieves the sales increase; reducing operating costs is not the value driver, but rather, eliminating the duplicate accounting department costs is a value driver. Value drivers should be specific actions that can be evaluated and measured by the organization. The M&A valuation proposal describes future cash flows based on assumptions describing how the business will operate, once the strategic *"To Be"* *state* is achieved. Key assumptions are those that are critical to the ultimate valuation of the transaction - the root cause of value that defines future cash flows. For an effective M&A transaction, assign specific actions to executives, and measure results to establish complete accountability.

Exhibit 3
Mergers & Acquisitions Summary
Weeks

TRANSACTION SUMMARY:	NOTES:	SUMMARY CASH FLOW: Description: (Millions $)	Resp	Year 1	2	3
Purchase Price	Millions $					
Cash	35.2	Reduce DSO	CFO	2.0		
Stock Value	20	Improved Invent turns	OPS	0.5	1.0	
Debt Assumed	5	Synergy - Sales	Sales	6.0	7.0	7.0
Subtotal	60.2	Synergy - Expenses	Mktng	2.0	2.0	2.0
Earnout	7	Synergy - Cap spend	Various	2.5	1.0	1.0
Total Cost	67.2	Total		13.0	11.0	10.0

THIS ACQUISITION WILL:
1. Increase Target Co. sales through expanded distribution.   **A**
2. Reduce Target Co. R&D spending by eliminating duplicate projects.   **B**
3. Reduce Target Co. IT spending - will be absorbed by our current infrastructure.   **C**

Newco P&L - Post Acquisition *(Year 1 - Millions $)*

	Baseline	Baseline	Nat'l Dist	Total
Sales	450.0	78.0	15.0	543.0
Gross Profit	225.0	40.0	10.0	275.0
SG&A				
Marketing			- 2.0	2.0
R&D				-
Outsourcing			- 0.5	0.5
Headcount			- 1.2	1.2
IT reduction			- 0.5	0.5
Total SG&A	-	-	- 4.2 -	4.2
Pretax Profit Impact	225.0	40.0	14.2	279.2

YEAR ONE OBJECTIVES:
1. Close Dallas Manufacturing.
2. Eliminate distributors in Central America.
3. Reduce headcount by 1,500.
4. Consolidate data systems into parent.
5. Reorganize R&D; eliminate duplicate projects; launch new products with sales of $4 million

NOTES:
A = Sales will increase due to broader distribution nationwide rather than regional.
B = Margins to increase to 67% due to no incremental overhead - only variable costs.
C = Target company duplicate advertising in trade journals.

Examine and understand the entire value chain of both the acquiring and the target business to identify the key value assumptions. Examine the entire value chain since any functional elements not considered in the assessment may be lost opportunities. The value chain is a master template that describes the functions required to be performed in any company, any size, and in any industry to be successful. Certain functions, such as Human Resources or Information Technology, support the entire business. Others, like manufacturing operations or logistics, directly produce value for the customers. In some companies, the functions may equate to departments, while in others -- - perhaps smaller companies - - functions may be combined in a single department (i.e. the manufacturing department will perform Inbound Logistics, Manufacturing Operations, and Outbound Logistics). Since there are 10 major elements in the value chain, the Due Diligence leader should do the following for each element:

- Validate the valuation assumptions;
- Summarize the potential upsides/downsides to the transaction;

- Summarize the integration and transition issues.

An example of the value chain follows:

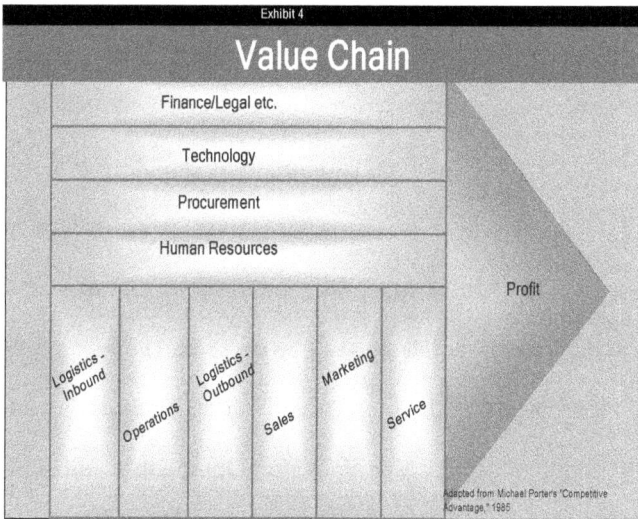

Exhibit 4

Value Chain

Finance/Legal etc.

Technology

Procurement

Human Resources

Profit

Logistics - Inbound

Operations

Logistics - Outbound

Sales

Marketing

Service

Adapted from Michael Porter's "Competitive Advantage," 1985

1.2.1 Critical Success Factors

Identify no more that 10 critical success factors to avoid diluting Company resources. Critical success factors will determine the acquisition's success or failure. Critical success factors are those few items that will allow the company to meet its strategic objectives. An example of a critical success factor is "consolidate and rationalize the combined company sales force," rather than a broad statement such as, "reduce selling expense."

1.2.2 Organization Structure/Culture/Personnel

Determine how the target company operates through its organization structure (identify the quality and number of personnel, extent of *outsourcing*, and assess the company culture) *and compare these features to the acquiring Company. Document the major differences and estimate the impact of any changes required to reach the desired future state.* Organization structure, culture, and related personnel

33

issues often cause integration failure. Failure could result from a poorly designed *"To Be"* organization, inadequate definition of authority and responsibility, culture and/or personality incompatibility. Early diagnosis of potential problems will help define required remediation costs, potential organizational and personnel changes, and changes to compensation and benefits required to be successful.

If, for example, the target company is managed informally with limited financial reporting, and the parent company is more formally managed - - requires weekly reporting and well-defined metrics - - a culture change and data systems change may be required to integrate the target successfully. This change to a more formal culture will disrupt the target company's business processes.

1.2.2.1 Organization Structure

Assess the organization structure considering compatibility and fit, to determine what, if any, adjustments will be required to reach the future state. Consider the number of organizational layers, the management span of control, centralized versus decentralized, union representation, special security clearances, and whether firms are structured geographically or functionally. Determine how the structures can be combined to reach the *"To Be"* state, and estimate the costs to integrate - severance, buy-out packages, increased compensation structures, organized labor impact etc.

1.2.2.2   Culture

Assess the target company organization and culture to validate assumptions related to structure and culture compatibility by completing an informal survey (See Exhibit 5) to document how the target company operates. Estimate the impact of significant culture differences considering employee training requirements, severance and hiring costs, customer and vendor turnover, and the inefficiencies inherent in extensive process change. Understand that parent companies that attempt to bring the target company performance standards to a higher level frequently fail, and overall lower standards erode total company performance to an unacceptable level.

Supplement the questionnaire in Exhibit 5 with observations by the transition teams of how the target company operates. Culture may differ among acquired business units depending on the local management, and the functions performed at the location. For example, a sales division may have a very different local culture than an R&D division.

Exhibit 5 provides a method to evaluate an organization or company. The key to the assessment isn't a rigid evaluation of every segment of a target company, but rather plot out your observations as you complete the Due Diligence review. Precision is not critical. As you review the various categories in the survey, a pattern will surface that allows you to interpret how the cultures will work together. In the case of *opposite cultures,* the survey may help you focus on priorities (note the *Rank* column) that can be resolved. For example, if the target is chaotic and highly fragmented, improved planning may be very helpful in blending the organizations.

Exhibit 5
Cultural Review

Management Orientation

REF	DESCRIPTION	Rank 1	2	3	4	5	DESCRIPTION
1	Rigid						Flexible
2	Directive						Participative
3	Bureaucratic						Entrepreneurial
4	Vacillating						Decisive
5	Cautions						Risk-taking
6	Reactive						Proactive
7	Suspicious						Trusting
8	Isolated						Involved
9	Closed-mouth						Open Minded
10	Task Oriented						People Oriented
11	Fragmented						Cohesive
12	Chaotic						Settled
13	Uncaring						Caring
14	Conflicting & Aggressive						Cooperative
15	Uninformative						Informative
16	Sr. Management Accessible						Isolation
17	Relatively Autocratic						Democratic

REF	DESCRIPTION	Rank Low 1	2	3	4	High 5
18	Clarity of Role Definition					
19	Team Spirit					
20	Value of Member in Organization					
21	Formalized Rules					
22	Free & Unconditional Info Sharing					
23	Reliant on Authority Rather than Task Experience					
24	Rewards based on contribution					
25	Formally structured Communication					
26	Interference From Head Office					
27	In this organization, individuals are expected to five first priority:			✔		
	a. Meeting the challenges of the individual task in which they are involved.					
	b. Cooperating with and attending to the needs of their fellow workers					
	c. Following the instructions of their superiors.					
	d. Acting with the parameters of their job description					

1.2.2.3   Personnel

Observe, question and interpret personnel performance.

Compare the personnel performance to the standards

expected when the combined company reaches the "To Be"

state. For example, if a manufacturing operation at the target company consists of technicians, and the *"To Be"* state requires more of an engineering orientation, valuation assumptions may reflect extensive personnel retraining or replacement. Document each shortcoming in the valuation process.

Identify key personnel during the Due Diligence review and determine the turnover risk. Key personnel are those constituents who are critical to the success of the transition to the *"To Be"* state. These individuals may not necessarily be retained long-term, but may be essential for the initial successful transition - e.g. their informal knowledge of the business operation. Consider special retention programs to reduce personnel turnover risk, and communicate the program to those affected by the decisions.

Evaluate personnel versus the performance standard expected when the "To Be" state is achieved. Identify gaps and determine if the gap is due to the quality of personnel, the experience, or the training provided. Determine what, if any, remedial action is required, and estimate the cost for valuation purposes.

1.2.2.4 Other people/constituents

Identify all functional activities. Examine the business relationships with constituents touched by the value chain to identify critical resources. Correlate the activity to the organization chart since outsourced processes may not be reflected on the organization chart. Review the formal and informal relationships. Some people/organizations, such as vendors, are not represented on the organization charts but are critical to the target Company's performance Include relationships with other third parties regulatory agencies such as the Food and Drug Administration, Department of Transportation, or the Department of Homeland Security; monitoring organizations such as Underwriter's Laboratories and International Standards Organization. A broad review of all constituents will ensure a thorough understanding of the target company.

1.2.3 Key Processes

Identify processes that are critical elements of the valuation, including outsourced processes, evaluate the quality of the processes compared to those expected in the future state of the combined company and *build the capital, and expense remediation costs into the valuation.* For example, if manufacturing quality at the combined Company is expected to be functioning at 6-sigma, and the target is only operating at 5-sigma, include the estimated costs to raise performance to the established standard.

Create a scorecard that evaluates all insourced and outsourced elements of the organization, using the master template of the value chain to guide the review. The scorecard should include people, processes, performance and capabilities of the target organization, and provide space for a preliminary and a final assessment of the personnel, structure and processes. Estimate remediation costs for any unacceptable ratings. Use as many subcategories as necessary to effectively display the target company assessment. In the following example, note that in some cases the acquiring company performance is below the expected *"To Be"* state:

					Exhibit 6		
					Due Diligence Reviewer's Guide		
		QUALITY ASSESSMENT					
Description	Priority Rank	AS IS			TO BE	Costs (000's $)	
		Company	Acquiring	Target	Transition Assessment	Comments	Annual Expense	Capital
RESEARCH & DEVELOPMENT Project development process Technology Personnel Intellectual property inventory	1	C	A	A	Overall target R&D department is superior to our co. in process, personnel and inventory of IP. To transition, our Co. must update our processes to mirror the target, and train personnel in the same performance standards as the target. Terminations of about 20% of our existing staff will be required. Additional $250k of capital required in our co. to match requirements. Expect that about 20% of our staff will not meet proficiency required to be successful	400	250

The above worksheet provides a template to evaluate each functional area in the Due Diligence review, and during the first hundred days. If there are major differences in the assessment, update the valuation estimate to reflect the changes required.

1.2.4   Physical Plant/Company Assets

Assess the plant/asset characteristics to ensure that the required "To Be" performance standards can be achieved, and include estimated remediation cost in the Valuation assumptions. Identify those assets that do not meet the expected standard and the estimated cost to raise them to an acceptable level of performance. Consider the quality and compatibility of equipment, the maintenance status, leased or purchased terms for all facilities and assets. Understand the quality of Intellectual Property and other intangible assets, and adjust the asset values to the current estimated value- e.g. customer lists or trade secrets.

1.2.5   Product

Assess the value of the product line (current and future product pipeline) considering its place in the product life cycle, validity of the intellectual property, and manufacturing

(sourcing) requirements.

There are three main concerns about product:

- o What is the status of the current product/service offering, which considers the life-cycle stage of the existing products - e.g. ... is there a future for this product, and scheduled product enhancements, given the competitive environment and global rapid technological advancements?

- o How valid is the product offering - e.g. can the intellectual property (patent) associated with the current product be challenged in the courts; can the product be produced as represented in the documentation provided by the seller?

- o Is the Company's product pipeline and new product development process worthy of investment - or an investment premium?

The judgment about each of these concerns could have a significant impact on the valuation of the Company, and how the products will fit with the acquiring Company's strategic goals.

1.2.6 Market

Assess the target Company's market, and market position to determine potential Company value. If the Target Company is in a new market segment, pay particular attention to the competitive environment, profitability ratios, market growth rates, and market segmentation. If in a new market segment, consider developing an in-depth market analysis to ensure that the Company's market strategy is achievable.

1.3 Review for upsides/downsides

Financial upsides and downsides relate to the initial valuation assumptions, and should consider all the elements discussed in the *Validate Assumptions* segment section 1.2:

- o Critical success factors;
- o Organization and personnel/constituents;
- o Process requirements;
- o Physical plant.

Functional executives and experts selected for the Due Diligence review team are responsible for the review, since opportunity often results from what is not easily visible. *These experts should be thoroughly familiar with the acquiring*

Company's organization, personnel, culture, plant and

processes, since value will be derived from combining with

the target company. Carefully review the entire value chain to

identify the upsides and downsides to the transaction.

Examples follow:

- o During a review of the physical manufacturing site,

  a highly qualified manufacturing expert may identify

  under-utilized equipment that is easily marketable,

  which could represent an upside to the transaction.

- o An expert may also identify inadequately

  maintained equipment, which may require refurbishing

  or replacement.

- o In the Research & Development (R&D) function, an

  expert may identify unused patents that have a market

  value in other non-competing industries.

- o An R&D expert may also identify inadequate

  procedures used to develop intellectual property,

  subjecting prior patents to challenge and invalidation.

Prepare summaries of Due Diligence items that identify the

issue, probable outcome or resolution, cost and time to

remediate. Exhibit 7 includes an example of a Due Diligence issue for a function, timing, type of issue, expected resolution and the individual responsible for resolution. Use a form similar to Exhibit 7 to establish accountability and as information included in the transaction valuation update.

As Due Diligence is completed, each Due Diligence team member will be able to agree with the following statement,

"The purpose of the acquisition can be fulfilled (... the "To Be" state...), and all costs and opportunities have been identified that could have a significant impact on the transaction."

If the team members cannot make that statement, *the acquisition team leader must decide if the open items are significant, if more work is required, or if the deal should be terminated.*

47

Exhibit 7
Due Diligence Issues
Company X

Function: Finance			Reference Issue:	
			Responsible:	
Timing:	Mark with X	Type	Mark with X	Reviewed:
				Date Open:
Immediate		Validation		Resolved:
One Year		Upside		
One Year +		Downside		
		Transition		

Description of Issue	Annual Exp	Capital
	(Millions US$)	

Resolution

1.4 Identify critical integration/transition issues

Review the analysis prepared related to understanding both businesses, including people/constituents, processes, plant/assets, products and market considerations to identify significant integration or transition issues. The tentative *"To Be"* state has been defined, each Due Diligence team member understands the purpose of the transaction and how the combined company - regardless of the extent of integration planned - will look. As the Due Diligence team members examine the target company functional areas and the ultimate acquisition goal, they should *identify integration and transition issues and opportunities, and summarize probable outcomes and costs/opportunities.*

Executive judgment and leadership are essential to a successful Due Diligence process. Integration and transition issues and summaries should include enough information to make a reasonable judgment as to probability of occurrence, cost, timing and resources required to complete the remediation. Each of these elements could have a significant impact on the valuation and price to be paid for the target company.

Some examples of integration issues:

- o Severance costs for redundant staff;
- o Training costs to upgrade staff to the required standard;
- o Refurbishing factory equipment to reach minimum required performance standards;
- o Sensitive union negotiations reviewing compensation and benefits;

- o Integration of different global information technology (IT) software and hardware systems;
- o Products reaching the end of their useful life;
- o A product pipeline void;
- o Dramatic changes in the competitive conditions - e.g. new market entrants; economic conditions.

1.5 Summarize All Due Diligence Issues

Summarize the expected financial and business impact of the issues identified during the validation, and present conclusions to the M&A leadership team. Include a summary of the upsides/downsides, and integration/transition issues. Due Diligence team leaders should summarize and review all significant Due Diligence issues, and review the information with the Acquisition Team leader to be sure that the deal valuation reflects the team's insight.

Exhibit 8
Due Diligence Issue Summary

Ref	Res	Validate	Upside	Downside	Integration	Description	Date		Financial Impact *(000's US $)*			
							Open	Resolve	Sales	Gross Margin	Expense	Capital
						Enter a brief description of the issue, and if multiple years, describe.			If multiple year impact, explain in description			

1.6 Project Plan

Exhibit 9 lists the major activities to be completed during the
Due Diligence process, leading up to actual deal completion.
Ideally, Due Diligence should be completed quickly - but
thoroughly enough to make a decision - since the target
company will be disrupted by the review, and the uncertainty of
a merger.

51

			Weeks											
Ref	Description	Resp	-4	-3	-2	-1	Closing	1	2	3	4	5	etc.
1.2	Validate valuation assumptions	ABB											
1.2.1	Identify critical success factors	JSC											
1.2.2	Define organization structure/culture/personnel	EDD											
1.2.2.1	Define organization structure												
1.2.2.2	Identify culture												
1.2.2.3	Identify key personnel												
1.2.2.4	Identify other key people/constituents												
1.2.3	Identify key processes												
1.2.4	Evaluate physical plant & key assets												

Exhibit 9
Mergers & Acquisitions Planning

INTEGRATION PLANNING

The accelerated schedule required high-level integration planning across all the companies acquired. The COO and the CFO concentrated initially on those items that were to be implemented immediately upon closing. The first priority Day One was to be sure that all the employees are in a payroll system, and all health benefits and critical fringe benefits were in place. Other Day One priorities include communications with key customers, and vendors. Communications with customers, vendors and employees were simplified to reinforce that, "While we have new owners, business will continue without any major changes." The communications plan was a one-page summary of bullet points, regardless of the audience. Matters, such as getting signs, business cards, company name changes, logos etc. could wait.

After Day One activities, organizing the back office would be the next major challenge. Since the headquarters staff was limited, the COO expected to use the most experienced individual among the acquired companies to manage each major function - Human Resources, Finance, Information Technology, Sales, Marketing and Manufacturing. Information Technology was important, since linking logistics among the warehouses was an important feature of the synergy.

Unfortunately, the roll-up timetable did not allow for either extensive integration planning. The accelerated schedule also did not allow for the team to properly understand executive capabilities in the acquired companies

The COO and CFO developed a high-level integration plan that blocked-out time periods and investment amounts (e.g. Upgrade IT systems - 90days, $200k; implement centralized, national warehouse - 6 months, $300k etc.) and broad performance goals.

2 The Executive Workshop – Framework

Overall, the integration/transition process includes three segments:

- o <u>Day One:</u> Identify activities that require immediate attention, such as compensation, benefits, cash management, insurance, contracts, communications, systems.

- o <u>First 100 days:</u> Confirm preliminary analysis and strategy developed before full access to the target company business and personnel. Early integration activities should concentrate on critical areas identified in the acquisition strategy.

- o <u>Second 100 days:</u> Continue plan execution, measure progress compared to the workshop goals, and reassess the overall strategy.

Conduct an Executive Workshop as soon as possible once the Due Diligence review is completed. Ideally, executives from both the acquirer and the target company should attend the workshop, although it is unlikely that the target company would allow its executives to begin thorough planning with the acquirer's executives until the deal is executed. Assemble key executives in the executive workshop to:

- o Confirm the acquisition objective, focus executive attention on the issues and broad plans for integration/transition (including reporting metrics);

- o Define a governance process to manage the integration/transition;

- o Identify and resolve schedule conflicts and priorities among the functions;

- o During the workshop, executives will review planned activities and define priorities, define communications and governance processes, and establish accountability for the transition team to deliver a completed project.

Workshop participants should include executives who represent the functional areas in the value chain for the companies involved in the transaction. Based on the team leader's judgment, the team should be composed of the best people, *not just the acquiring company executives.* The workshop leader will coordinate the meeting by first reviewing each participant's work prior to the workshop to better understand the issues, prioritize the agenda items based on importance, and facilitate the process.

The workshop agenda will require one-to-two days, depending on the transaction size and complexity. *The facilitator will initially review the integration process guidelines, team organization structure, and the companies' current and "To Be" state.* The *"To Be"* state will be time scaled to reflect major events, such as year-one company goals.

Throughout the executive workshop, executives will review functional assessments and integration plans, share plans about how the activities will be coordinated among functions, and establish their vision for the *"To Be"* business. Executives will develop the integration master plan, measurable business goals including forecast P&Ls, Balance Sheets and Cash Flow, Capital spending, and other metrics unique to each transaction - i.e. headcount, sales per headcount, and production targets.

The executive workshop is not a process for the executives to develop their plans, but rather a process to review their assessments and functional plans - - "As Is" today, the projected "To Be" state, and high-level transition plans - - and coordinate major events among all the functions in all the companies. Before the workshop, each executive will develop and review the completed plans with their functional teams.

The facilitator will review the executives' plans before the workshop to understand each function's plans. After completing the one/two-day workshop, integration plans will be refined to reflect the group conclusions during the week following the workshop. The team will develop financial summaries and other metrics in the subsequent week. Executives will define reporting and future communications during the workshop. The workshop and outcomes should proceed as follows:

- o Facilitator to learn the deal: *2-3 days in advance*

- o Workshop activity: *1-2 days*
- o Refine integration plans: *1 week*
- o Refine financial and metrics: *1 week*
- o Execution: *Less than 1 year*

The facilitator should become familiar with the deal elements, and all available background related to Due Diligence, business forecasts, issues and opportunities. This background will allow the facilitator to focus on the most important issues.

Deal complexity will determine the length of the workshop, but ideally, the workshop will not be longer than two days. If the integration is too complex to finish in a two-day workshop, have mini workshops in advance - e.g. with the source of complexity such as Manufacturing Operations - to summarize the issues.

Once the actual workshop is finished, functional executives often refine their plans as they have learned more about the transition priorities, as well as the costs and benefits of the overall transaction. The executives should review the adjustments with the functional teams to develop consensus. This should be completed in the first week after the workshop.

The workshop facilitator should assemble the modified plans and update the deal summaries to reflect the current planning status. Ideally, changes made to early plans will be consistent with guidelines developed at the workshop, and another executive workshop will not be required. If extensive changes are made, the facilitator should schedule a brief meeting to gain consensus on new objectives.

Exhibit 10 below describes the activities and deliverables post-closing. During the workshop, each element of analysis and deliverable will be prepared based on information known pre-deal, since it is *unlikely* that a seller will allow full and complete access to all personnel, processes, customers and vendors. Once the deal is closed, the team should validate assumptions and plans.

Exhibit 10

	First 100 Days		Second 100 Days	
Day One	Analysis & Strategy	Detail Design, Build & Execute	Sustain & Harvest Benefits	Synergy
Analyze & Execute **A** **s** **s** **e** **s** **s** **&** **P** **l** **a** **n**	· Understand keys to value · Assess hi-level business model · Review organization & structure · Review comp & bonus/ fringe · Review processes & systems · Prepare hi-level gap analysis · Prioritize activities	· Design process flows · Define tech & facilities · ID & train personnel · Relentless executionUnderstand keys to value	· '100' day status check · Reassess priorities · Align activities to priorities	· '200' day status check · Strategic assessment
Execute **E** **x** **e** **c** **u** **t** **e**	· Organization & structure · Comp & bonus plans: fringe · Personnel alignment · Prioritized processes & systems · Implementation timetable · Financial assessment · Contingency plans · Communications strategy	· Detail project plan · Procedures developed · Personnel trained · Active project management & reporting · Processes implemented · Communications strategy execution · Contingency planning	· Detailed status review · Priority assessment · Financial assessment · Updated project plan	· Strategic assessment

...Deliverables ...

2.1 Facilitator review

The facilitator should understand the overall transaction as a basis for the functional presentations. The high-level introduction will summarize key elements of the deal, costs, significant transition activity, and contingency plans. Later in the workshop, other executives will share their detailed functional plans to ensure a well-coordinated process.

2.1.1 Review/modify/confirm the high-level business model and financial goals

The facilitator will present the high-level business model that describes the current state and the proposed or "To Be" *state of the companies.* The introduction will establish a common understanding of the *"To Be"* state, and identify reporting metrics that are significant to the business, such as gross margins, SG&A ratios, cash flows, and asset intensity. It will also help to identify obstacles in reaching the *"To Be"* state. Obstacles to completion should either be resolved, or managed using an open items summary. The high-level business model consists of two elements:

- **Structure:** The structure describes the companies' physical attributes at each location. For example, a company location will include functions such as Sales Operations, Customer Service, Human Resources and so forth, and a description of the facilities themselves.

- **Responsibilities:** Define the organization role at each location, separated between strategic leadership and tactical performance. Briefly outline the strategic and tactical requirements.

Once requirements for the high-level business model are defined, identify key personnel, organization structure, and business processes. The business model presents the acquisition's strategic goal. *Prepare the model using input from key executives. The overall model will be the framework that other executives use to demonstrate fit within the new strategy.* The business model will include the company description - - physical sites, number of employees, and key financial metrics, such as return on sales, ROI, growth expectations. The model will also include a broad description of how the business will operate, using a high-level organization chart and description of authority and responsibilities. Note in Exhibit 11 that certain functions were previously completed in Company A (Customer Service, Accounting, IT, Sales, and Marketing) have now been combined into the Revised Company B. Only Human Resource and Manufacturing will continue in the Revised Company A.

Exhibit 11

Organization Structure

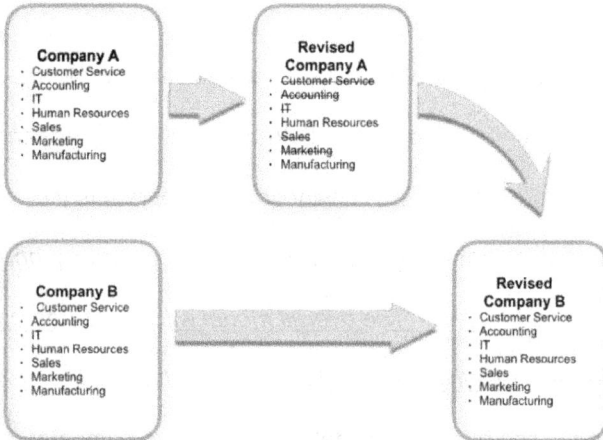

Company A
- Customer Service
- Accounting
- IT
- Human Resources
- Sales
- Marketing
- Manufacturing

Revised Company A
- Customer Service
- Accounting
- IT
- Human Resources
- Sales
- Marketing
- Manufacturing

Company B
- Customer Service
- Accounting
- IT
- Human Resources
- Sales
- Marketing
- Manufacturing

Revised Company B
- Customer Service
- Accounting
- IT
- Human Resources
- Sales
- Marketing
- Manufacturing

2.1.2 Confirm the keys to valuation

The facilitator will prepare the acquisition summary including the strategic goal, proforma financial statements and highlights, incremental integration costs, and critical success factors that will guide the integration/transition process.

	Exhibit 12		
	Mergers & Acquisitions Summary		
Weeks			

TRANSACTION SUMMARY: NOTES:

Purchase Price	Millions $
Cash	35.2
Stock Value	20
Debt Assumed	5
Subtotal	60.2
Earnout	7
Total Cost	67.2

SUMMARY CASH FLOW:
Description: (Millions $)

	Resp	Year 1	Year 2	Year 3
Reduce DSO	CFO	2.0		
Improved Invent turns	OPS	0.5	1.0	
Synergy - Sales	Sales	6.0	7.0	7.0
Synergy - Expenses	Mktng	2.0	2.0	2.0
Synergy - Cap spend	Various	2.5	1.0	1.0
Total		13.0	11.0	10.0

THIS ACQUISITION WILL:
1. Increase Target Co. sales through expanded distribution. **A**
2. Reduce Target Co. R&D spending by eliminating duplicate projects. **B**
3. Reduce Target Co. IT spending - will be absorbed by our current infrastructure. **C**

YEAR ONE OBJECTIVES:
1. Close Dallas Manufacturing.
2. Eliminate distributors in Central America.
3. Reduce headcount by 1,500.
4. Consolidate data systems into parent.
5. Reorganize R&D; eliminate duplicate projects; launch new products with sales of $4 million

Newco P&L - Post Acquisition (Year 1 - Millions $)

	Baseline	Baseline	Nat'l Dist	Total
Sales	450.0	78.0	15.0	543.0
Gross Profit	225.0	40.0	10.0	275.0
SG&A				
Marketing			- 2.0	2.0
R&D				-
Outsourcing			- 0.5	0.5
Headcount			- 1.2	1.2
IT reduction			- 0.5	0.5
Total SG&A	-	-	4.2	4.2
Pretax Profit Impact	225.0	40.0	14.2	279.2

NOTES:
A = Sales will increase due to broader distribution nationwide rather than regional.
B = Margins to increase to 67% due to no incremental=l overhead - only variable costs.
C = Target company duplicate advertising in trade journals.

2.1.3 Review and Present the Complete value chain

Workshop attendees will review the entire value chain to share their vision of the future Company. They will develop and approve the transition plans, and through the business plan review and coordination process, develop creative contingency plans to achieve acquisition goals. It is possible that one executive's plans will not be easily implemented. For example, the Vice President - Sales may require a fully implemented Customer Resource Management (CRM) package by the first quarter, but this may not be a feasible goal to the IT department. Problem solving capabilities of the best executives attending the workshop will develop innovative solutions to conflicts and create a consensus plan, including contingency plans that ensure the success of the merger. See Exhibit 4 for a more complete description of the value chain.

2.1.4 Financial cost estimates

Costs and investment decisions should be evaluated based on the impact to reach the planned *"To Be"* state.

WARNING - Executives responsible for routine activities may consider each cost in relation to their annual budget, rather than in relation to the investment in the merger. Executives may be reluctant to invest $500,000 in new systems in the normal course of business, but when the investment is considered as protecting a $50 million acquisition, the decision would be made. Summarize financial results, including cost estimates for the following:

o   Hidden costs include as much as 50 percent inefficiency for both organizations. Costs reflecting lost customers, sales and profitability may also be significant. Evaluate expense investments using this as a basis of comparison. For example, if hiring a $25,000 consultant will accelerate the integration by two months, saving $50,000 of duplicate resources, the investment is justified.

o   Incurred costs to execute the integration process can include both capital and expense items, which should be identified during the Due Diligence, integration planning, and execution.

     o   Baseline costs exist if nothing is changed. For example, a merged company with two identical IT departments would include all costs in the baseline costs.

The financial statements include baseline spending (financial results before the combination), and the estimated combined entity. The sum of the two are not necessarily equal to the *"To Be"* state. *Identify major changes from current state and hold executives accountable for delivering the expected results.*

Establish accountability over both the P&L and balance sheet in the planning to ensure that the company achieves the acquisition goals.

2.1.5 Summarize/assess key personnel/ constituents

The integration team will Identify key personnel and positions within the organization, and discuss plans to retain them, recognizing that certain matters should remain confidential. Summarize expected key personnel losses or major gaps in the organizations to be resolved during the workshop. Key personnel/constituents include any person or organization that interacts with either company - e.g. key vendors.

2.1.6 Summarize the high level plans

Outline the high-level activities that will be required to reach the future state. Examples of the high-level issues may include replacing data systems, implementing *Lean Manufacturing* concepts, eliminating factories or replacing functional areas with outside resources. This segment of the workshop will educate the participants about the major points of change, and allow them to view their functions as they relate to the total company. For example, if the company were replacing all data systems in the next 12-18 months, it would be foolish to upgrade existing systems to a more current version of the old software.

2.1.7 Develop a communications strategy/plan

Outline a preliminary communications strategy and communications plan. The communications plan should include constituents served, major events planned, mode and frequency of communication. The plan will sensitize executives to the communication approach and strategy so that the workshop can build on the plan as issues develop.

2.1.8 Develop contingency plans

Regardless of how thorough the pre-planning, actual results are seldom achieved as planned. *At the conclusion of the workshop, the executive team will develop contingency plans that include activities, names, dates and milestones to activate the contingency plans to assure delivery of the acquisition goals.*

2.2 Participants/Attendees

Select workshop participants who can effectively assess, plan, and execute the integration process. The executive leaders who will implement the transition/integration plan may be from either the buyer or the target organization, but should include only the best executives regardless of prior company affiliation, as determined by the executive responsible for the integration project. Consider executives from all organizations as participants. The workshop team should be limited to 15 or fewer senior executives who wield enough organizational power to make decisions and allocate resources to the project as required. If executives do not have the skills required to effectively plan and execute the assessment and planning, supplement their knowledge with specialists to achieve the goal.

2.2.1 Leaders – both sides of the transaction

The CEO or Chairman of the Board will select executive attendees, based on skills required, experience and anticipated business priorities. Teams should include executives from both organizations, if possible, to avoid the appearance of a dominant organization. There must be a single agenda, and a common purpose to achieve integration success.

2.2.2 Integration teams: only the best people

Select the best personnel on the broader integration teams to assess the goals, develop the creative plans to achieve the goals, and share their information with other executives at the workshop. The workshop will then empower these executives in their transitional role and in the future organization.

2.3 Executive Advocates

Assign Executive Advocates (EA) to be responsible for segments of the transition, including people, processes and plant/assets to ensure there are no gaps in performance in any functional areas. Executive advocates are those executives who are personally accountable for the success of specific elements of the transition. The EA will coordinate the assessment, planning and execution of any transition activities. The EA will also be responsible for communications - - listening -- as well as outbound communications for all constituents within the defined area.

Publish the list of EA's, using a newsletter, organization charts, and/or websites so that constituent questions or problems are resolved on a timely basis. For example, if the VP of Human Resources is the Executive Advocate, for Human Resources, the EA is responsible for the physical assets, such as adequate computer equipment, office space, and software accessibility, the processes within that responsibility, as well as all the people issues involved in the Human Resources function. The following items are the EA responsibility:

72

o People/constituents: Any group or organization touched by either organization, including employees (current/retired), consultants, outsourcing organizations, vendors, governmental or regulatory agencies Etc.

o Processes/activities: Any process or activity completed by either organization, anywhere in the business, including processes and activities performed by outside organizations.

o Plant/assets: Any physical plant or asset (tangible or intangible) whether directly controlled or owned by either organization, or rented/leased or used by the organization.

2.3.1 Identify constituents

Define people/constituents, which include any individuals, groups or organizations touched by the acquiring or target company. This includes employees (current/retired), consultants, outsourcing organizations, vendors, governmental or regulatory agencies Etc.

Executives responsible for the support functions, such as Finance or Human Resources, serve a dual role since their functional responsibilities may span the entire company. A finance executive is therefore responsible for financial controls, reporting and planning in all functional areas, not just within the finance function.

2.3.2 Related processes

Identify all related processes/activities, which include those completed by either organization, anywhere in the course of business. This includes processes and activities performed by outside organizations.

2.4 Establish rules of governance

Establish the rules of governance. This should include the overall management process, reporting, accountabilities, decision processes, approval levels, hiring/firing personnel, contract negotiations, purchasing authority, project approvals, and communications. The facilitator will establish the rules with the CEO/Chairman in advance, and review the rules with the leadership team to ensure that executives understand the process and expectations.

2.4.1 Define integration leadership

Determine the integration team leadership based on the acquisition's strategic objectives and the best-qualified personnel to complete the job. Team selection should be purpose driven, and not politically driven. Leadership during the transition and integration process may differ from the day-to-day business management due to the acquisition strategic priorities. If, for example, R&D intellectual property transfer is critical, a technical expert may have a leading role in the integration. Assign the best people to roles to ensure the merger success. If necessary, hire an outside consultant to manage the successful transition. During the integration period, this individual may have significant authority within the organization, since the individual may manage the entire integration.

2.4.2 Structure/organization

Develop guidelines before the meeting, to manage the interim structure and organization throughout the integration

75

project. The structure and organization will define the

operating principles used throughout the integration process,

such as authority to spend expense or capital, hiring/firing,

compensation and bonus, operational approvals authority.

Exhibit 13 displays the high-level organization and the

responsibilities separated between strategic and tactical. All

functional areas, regardless of their importance before the

combination, will participate to avoid missed opportunities.

Exhibit 13

High Level Business Model

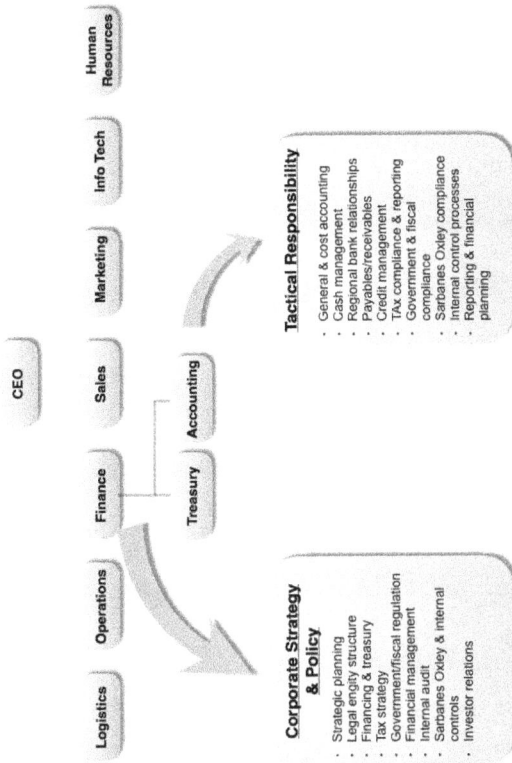

CEO

Logistics | Operations | Finance | Sales | Marketing | Info Tech | Human Resources

Treasury | Accounting

Corporate Strategy & Policy

· Strategic planning
· Legal engity structure
· Financing & treasury
· Tax strategy
· Government/fiscal regulation
· Financial management
· Internal audit
· Sarbanes Oxley & internal controls
· Investor relations

Tactical Responsibility

· General & cost accounting
· Cash management
· Regional bank relationships
· Payables/receivables
· Credit management
· Tax compliance & reporting
· Government & fiscal compliance
· Sarbanes Oxley compliance
· Internal control processes
· Reporting & financial planning

77

In the example, activities are separated between Strategic and Tactical. Focus on both long and short term objectives when developing the organization, since the longer-term perspective will help you make better strategic decisions. One executive may prepare the summary for multiple functions - e.g. logistics, and operations. While the number of entries in either the strategic or the tactical responsibilities may vary, focus on key items to avoid diluting resources. Prepare one summary for each functional area. Executives may prepare similar, additional lower level summaries for locations around the globe if they are significant to the integrated "To Be" company.

Freeze all headcount changes, all salary changes, promotions, new hires or reorganizations until both organizations have been reviewed to identify if any major changes will occur with the transition. You do not want to promote individuals and then terminate as redundant two months later.

2.4.2.1   Decision processes

Identify the processes that will be affected by the integration effort, and establish rules to be followed during the integration process. The best way to identify such processes is to work with the employees that actually perform the activity, who also understand the "To Be" state. Develop procedures for significant processes required during the integration such as hiring/firing, compensation, bonuses, stock options, purchases of expense/capital, and customer trade terms. Prepare a matrix of all affected procedures similar to Exhibit 14, to be sure that there are no control gaps.

Exhibit 14 Decision Processes/Authority								
Vice President Company			Director Company			Manager Company		
A	B	Newco	A	B	Newco	A	B	Newco
Human Resources								
Hiring ✓								
- In Plan ✓	✓		✓	✓				
- Outside Plan ✓								
Firing ✓			✓	✓				
Raises								
- Scheduled	✓		✓	✓		✓	✓	
- Non-Scheduled ✓								
Bonus		✓						
Special Incentives		✓						
Stock Options		✓						
Promotions ✓								
Vacations ✓								
Holidays		✓						

79

2.4.2.2   Reporting frequency, content, and audience

Determine the frequency, content and audience for reporting.
Develop reporting requirements based on the integration
objectives, and the "To Be" state of the companies as well as
reporting requirements to manage the day-to-day business.

- o *Formally monitor critical short and long cycle*
  metrics. Monitor short-cycle metrics daily or
  weekly as required. This may include sales,
  order flow, cash reporting and borrowing,
  headcount, hiring/firing, capital spending,
  project spending and progress. Formally
  monitor longer cycle activities such as new
  product development, plant closures, and
  product sourcing changes at the executive level
  monthly.

- o *Define integration/transition goals in sufficient*
  detail to establish metrics and accountabilities
  throughout the organization. Report content
  should reflect the goals and the responsibility
  levels within the organization. For example,
  daily cash reporting should display total cash

received at the executive level. However, cash receipts may also be summarized by region in lower level reports, so that the regional executives can be measured against goals. Sales orders may be total or by product line at the executive level, while accountabilities may also be established at the product management level for mid-level executives. Mid-level executives may receive daily order reports, while senior executives may receive weekly or monthly activity reports.

o   Audience: *Restrict report distribution to those that need the information* to manage effectively. Avoid the temptation to expand the report distribution to create a status symbol for those receiving the reports.

Use two types of reporting to manage the integration:

o   Develop financial reports that include:

▪   Integration project reporting for incremental capital and expense spending. During the planning process, executives will identify

incremental spending for outside assistance,

registration fees, and licensing. Include these

estimates in forecasted financial results, and

establish executive accountability.

- Essential <u>financial information that relates</u>

  <u>to the total company project such as P&Ls,</u>

  <u>Balance Sheet, and financial performance</u>

  <u>metrics</u> including DSO, and Inventory Turns.

  P&L and Balance Sheet performance metrics

  can be helpful to manage synergy,

  incremental sales, and improvements in

  balance sheet metrics for the entire company.

o   Develop <u>project reporting within the functional</u>

  <u>teams, and summary reporting to the</u>

  <u>Integration/Transition teams</u>. At each progress

  review, the leaders should confirm that, "The

  project will be completed on schedule." When

  leaders do not expect to achieve plan

  performance, they should outline the actions

  required to reach the plan schedule, and then

fully integrate any major schedule changes into the overall project schedule.

2.4.2.3 Communications: Formal & Informal

Plan a total communications strategy to both report on progress and maintain an open and free flow of information to those requiring it. Good communications are essential to the integration process, and formal reporting will assist in that process. Communications are both outbound and inbound - listening. Develop a master communications matrix during the planning process to communicate goals and accomplishments to your constituents. As you develop and execute the plan, inform your constituents, and monitor feedback throughout the integration process. Integration leadership and their teams must observe and listen to the constituents. The communications planning matrix can use one axis to define the information requirements, and the other to define frequency and audience. As you plan the communications matrix, identify noteworthy events and activities and manage the flow of information in a fair and responsible manner to keep your constituents informed. Exhibit 15 includes many points of information. The objective is to understand the overall communications process, and the numerous messages that are expected in the near future. In this case, the "$" is used to indicate the magnitude of the announcement. More "$" identify more significant communications. Probability describes the likelihood of the activity actually occurring and the timing, which becomes less precise the further into the future that we project.

				Exhibit 15 Communications Planning - Content									
Description	Resp	Priority	Probability	Jan				Feb				Mar	
				1	2	3	4	1	2	3	4	1	2
Plant closure													
Chicago	JCC	A	100%		$$$								
Atlanta	MRF	A	100%							$$$			
Facility expansion													
New Sales Offices													
New Orleans	AFR	B	90%							$			
Charlotte	AFR	C	50%			$$							

2.4.3   Review the Deal

The workshop leader will present, to all workshop participants, a high-level deal transaction summary including all-important information such as investment summary, assumptions, expectations, timing, and key measures. Key measures can include such items as sales, earnings, gross margins, headcount, and capital spending. Throughout the workshop, executives will present their function's plans, to ensure consistency with the overall company investment goal. Each deal summary will include different information, because each deal will have unique critical items. Distribute the transaction summary to the executive teams to establish executive alignment, which is essential for success.

Three examples of deal summaries follow:

- o Acquisition Proposal - - High-level summary that describes the heart of the transaction, such as key elements of valuation, financial projections, key employees, and approximate timeline.

- o Key deliverables and assigned accountabilities.

- o Integration planning cost details.

Exhibit 16
Mergers & Acquisitions Summary
Weeks

TRANSACTION SUMMARY: NOTES:

Purchase Price	Millions $
Cash	35.2
Stock Value	20
Debt Assumed	5
Subtotal	60.2
Earnout	7
Total Cost	67.2

SUMMARY CASH FLOW: Description: *(Millions $)*	Resp	Year 1	2	3
Reduce DSO	CFO	2.0		
Improved Invent turns	OPS	0.5	1.0	
Synergy - Sales	Sales	6.0	7.0	7.0
Synergy - Expenses	Mktng	2.0	2.0	2.0
Synergy - Cap spend	Various	2.5	1.0	1.0
Total		**13.0**	**11.0**	**10.0**

THIS ACQUISITION WILL:

1. Increase Target Co. sales through expanded distribution. **A**

2. Reduce Target Co. R&D spending by eliminating duplicate projects. **B**

3. Reduce Target Co. IT spending - will be absorbed by our current infrastructure. **C**

YEAR ONE OBJECTIVES:

1. Close Dallas Manufacturing.
2. Eliminate distributors in Central America.
3. Reduce headcount by 1,500.
4. Consolidate data systems into parent.
5. Reorganize R&D; eliminate duplicate projects; launch new products with sales of $4 million

Newco P&L - Post Acquisition *(Year 1 - Millions $)*

	Baseline	Baseline	Nat'l Dist	Total
Sales	450.0	78.0	15.0	543.0
Gross Profit	225.0	40.0	10.0	275.0
SG&A				
Marketing		-	2.0	2.0
R&D			-	-
Outsourcing		-	0.5	0.5
Headcount		-	1.2	1.2
IT reduction		-	0.5	0.5
Total SG&A	-	-	4.2	4.2
Pretax Profit Impact	**225.0**	**40.0**	**14.2**	**279.2**

NOTES:

A = Sales will increase due to broader distribution nationwide rather than regional.

B = Margins to increase to 67% due to no incremental overhead - only variable costs.

C = Target company duplicate advertising in trade journals.

Description	Company			New Co	Notes	Responsibility
	A	B	A+B			
Operating Assets (Net of Depreciation)	450.0	700.0	1,150.0	900.0	1	Manufacturing
Employees	350.0	400.0	750.0	600.0		
P&L						
Sales	700.0	900.0	1,600.0	1,450.0	2	Sales
Gross Profit	400.0	600.0	1,000.0	1,000.0	3	Manufacturing
% to Sales	*57%*	*67%*	*63%*	*69%*		
Expenses						
Selling	75.0	150.0	225.0	200.0		
Marketing	75.0	75.0	150.0	125.0	4	Marketing
R&D	70.0	120.0	190.0	200.0		
Administration	45.0	60.0	105.0	75.0	5	Finance
Total Expenses	265.0	405.0	670.0	600.0		
Pretax Earnings	135.0	195.0	330.0	400.0		

This chart represents a financial summary of the benefits of synergy. The ideal method to size the company is to look at the industry, products, processes, and to then determine the best company of the future - the "To Be". Review should not be influenced by the composition or structure of the current company.

Notes:
1 = Disposition of the LA manufacturing facility
2 = VP of Sales to eliminate products with sales less than $1 million, and Gross Margin of   less than 30 percent
3 = Manufacturing to eliminate the LA manufacturing facility and 150 employees.
4 = Marketing to eliminate Public Relations in the target company.
5 = Finance to eliminate duplicate Information Systems function.

Exhibit 18

Integration Planning Costs & Capital
(Millions $)

Description	Total Costs			Monthly	Notes
	Estimate	Minimum	Maximum	Run Rate	
P&L					
Base Costs					
Legal					
Fees	0.5	0.3	0.7	0.2	A
Travel	0.1	0.1	0.1	0.1	
Registrations/filings	0.1	0.1	0.1		
Licenses	0.1	0.1	0.1		
Finance					
Fees	0.3	0.2	0.4	0.1	
Travel	0.1	0.1	0.1		
Registrations	0.1	0.1	0.1		
Manufacturing					
Engineering	0.4	0.3	0.8	0.1	
Temporaries	0.3	0.3	0.4	0.1	
Inefficiencies					
Manufacturing	1.5	1.0	2.0	0.5	B
Distribution	0.2	0.2	0.3		
MIS	0.3	0.3	0.8	0.1	
Total P&L - Costs	**4.0**	**3.1**	**5.9**	**1.2**	
CAPITAL					
Software Licenses	0.2	-	0.5	n/a	
MIS - Hardware	0.4	0.2	1.5	n/a	
Total Capital	**0.6**	**0.2**	**2.0**		

Notes:
- Estimates are very broad ... precision is not required at this point, but there should be a reasonable level of accountability.
- Monthly run rate will assist in comparison of trade-offs with out-of-pocket costs, compared to savings to accelerate the project.
- Cost estimates will be prepared by functional exec responsible for the area, and will be used to measure performance.
- Inefficiency can be major cost, and is often overlooked. This does not capture the market cost of disrupted customers.
- Minimum/maximum/estimated costs frame the potential impact of the entire transaction.
- Capital estimates assist in Cash Flow planning.

Estimates are based on a 90-day transition for the integration.

A = Represents out-of-pocket costs for incremental legal... and monthly run rate if the process is prolonged.
B = Represents estimated lost efficiency due to key manufacturing personnel travel to target company & not attending to current schedule.

2.4.3.1 Transaction Summary

Prepare a transaction summary that briefly describes the deal's strategic objective, the "To Be" state, and any important elements of the "To Be" state. For example, the *"To Be"* state may be described in one year and then again in three years if significant change will be made during that period. Be brief, but with sufficient detail so that the company goals are understood by workshop attendees.

2.4.3.2 Purpose

Describe the deal's strategic objective and summarize the *"To Be"* state and its important elements. For example, the *"To Be"* state may be described in one year, two years and three years.

2.4.3.3 People

Identify critical people/constituents and activities at both companies. "People" includes critical vendors, key customers, and regulatory agencies such as the Food and Drug Administration (FDA) or the Department of Transportation (DOT). Also, identify potential constituents, such as new customers, new customer classes, or new

89

vendors who may become critical due to the combination of the companies. For example, if the combined company will become a global service provider, additional legal counsel or tax expertise may be required.

2.4.3.4   Processes

Summarize all critical processes, whether internal or outsourced. Critical processes are those that are essential to make the acquisition successful. For example, perfecting the patent on a unique new product could be an essential process that would cause the deal to falter if not properly managed.

2.4.3.5   Plant/Assets

Identify all significant plant and assets including all physical and intangible assets, whether owned, leased or used, if the assets are used in the business. For example, if an airport or shipping facility in close proximity to a production facility were essential to timely delivery of product, the facility would be an essential element of the transaction summary.

2.4.3.6   Key elements of valuation

Summarize the key valuation elements. Aim for fewer than 10 elements at the highest level that will make the transaction successful.

2.4.3.7 Known upsides/downsides

Develop contingency plans that describe alternate ways to achieve the acquisition goals. These plans will initially be developed during the Due Diligence process, and will be expanded during the executive workshop as each executive reviews their transition plans and risk assessments.

2.4.4 Review the Operations/Functions – Functional Executive

After the high-level review *by the* workshop facilitator, *each executive will review the operations under their direct control.* Since the only source of information about the acquired company is that obtained during the pre-deal process and Due Diligence review, plans presented are still preliminary, pending further review starting on Day One. *Assign responsibility for every person (constituent), process (activity), and plant (asset) to an executive to manage to the "To Be" state.* Executives should summarize:

- o The "As Is" business,

- o The "To Be" state,

- o The plans to achieve that goal.

See examples of standard review templates for the presentation in Exhibit 19. *Assign each executive's review time based on importance to achieving the acquisition goal.* For example, accounting may have a minor impact on the success of the transaction, while the sales force will be essential. The Integration executive may allocate the sales function two hours for review, while the finance function will receive 30 minutes since there may be less business risk in the finance function. The individual executive review will ensure organizational alignment. If executives disagree about the goals and structure, differences will be resolved at this time.

This segment of the workshop will be similar to the high-level summary, and will include information from each executive such as:

- Confirmed valuation assumptions

- High-level business model (see Exhibit 13)

- Process review and changes required

- Organization structure and key constituents

- Keys to valuation as applicable to the functions

- Gap analysis

- Financial summaries

2.4.4.1 Entire value chain by function

Functional executives will review their portion of the critical value chain elements to ensure agreement among the workshop executives. During the workshop, executives will review up to 10 summaries. They will review one summary for each element of the value chain depicted in Exhibit 4.

2.4.4.1.1 Confirm valuation assumptions

93

Each executive will review the critical valuation assumptions

as they relate to their function to ensure that all executives

have a thorough and common understanding of the deal. For

example, if a key to valuation is increasing manufacturing

throughput by 25 % without any increase in manufacturing

overhead, the responsible executive should state that the

saving is achievable. Functions that are not essential

elements of the valuation will work to achieve the overall

acquisition goal.

2.4.4.1.2   "To Be" state

Prepare a summary of the "To Be" state of the combined

operations at specific and significant time intervals.

Important time intervals may be at 100 days, six months, and

one year. These intervals will vary with each transaction.

Identify factors that are measurable and consistent with the

overall acquisition strategy.   For example, if a key to

valuation is increasing manufacturing throughput by 25 %

within 12 months, without any increase in manufacturing

overhead, the responsible executive should state that the

savings are achievable.

2.4.4.1.3   High Level Business Model

94

While considering confidential matters, each executive will review the personnel/organization, and constituency. Factors such as critical personnel, or other constituents, organization size and structure, changes in compensation, benefits, and expanded and reduced staff levels should be discussed, if critical. Each executive will summarize the *"As Is"*, and the *"To Be"* organization, and review transition plans to reach the goal. During this process, executives will identify and discuss organizational or constituency gaps and plans to resolve the gap through hiring, improving processes, or investing in plant/assets to eliminate the gap. For example, if the manufacturing organization in the acquired company does not use Computer Assisted Design/Manufacturing (CAD/CAM) equipment, add CAD/CAM trained engineers to the organization to raise the performance standards at the target company.

Exhibit 19
Functional GAP Analysis

Gap Analysis - Finance *As Is* transition *To Be*		
Notes	1	2
	(Millions US $)	

Personnel

US Operations

Global Credit Manager	0.2	0.2

Asia

Business Analysts	0.2	0.3
Credit Manager	0.1	0.1
Internal Control Specialist		
Cost Accountants (4)		0.2
Sub-total	0.3	0.6
Market Adjustments	0.1	0.1
Total Personnel	0.6	0.9

Processes

US Operations

Credit Management Systems	0.1	
Training	0.1	
Credit Assessment Reporting	0.1	0.1
	0.3	0.1

Capital

PC's	0.3	0.1

2.4.4.1.4   Processes (... facilities, assets etc.)

The executives will discuss each process in both the "As Is" and the "To Be" state and identify integration issues and performance gaps. They will discuss factors that are significant to the integration, or items that are essential for other executives to understand. *Prepare gap analyses that identify the issues and the proposed solutions to the gap*

such as capital, work force, and training. In the

manufacturing example, the CAD/CAM process is a gap,

which may require outsourcing; or additional internal staff,

training and capital equipment.

A matrix identifying significant processes used in the

organizations will highlight opportunities for change. The

matrix can include descriptions of the processes, assessment

of the quality or robust capabilities, and compatibility.

Exhibit 20
Process Summary Analysis
Purchasing

| | US Operations | | | | Offshore | | |
	Dallas	Chicago	Dayton	Miami	Paris	London	Madrid
Contract Administration							
Local Contracts							
Services	A,2				B,2	A,1	A,1
Products	A,1				B,2	A,1	A,1
Global Contracts							
Commodity Products			B,1				
Specialty Products							
Electrical		A,1					
Purchasing							
Services				B,3			
Products							
Capital			A,1			B,1	
Supplies							

A = Excellent   1 = Fully Compatible
B = Acceptable   2 = Acceptable
C = Substandard   3 = Incompatible

2.4.4.1.5   Capital/incremental spending

The executive will identify the preliminary incremental

capital/expense, carefully considering confidential matters that should not be disclosed - e.g. individual performance incentives. Each executive will review his/her capital/incremental spending including significant elements required to achieve the *"To Be"* state. These elements could include spending amount, timing, type of spending such as lease, capital spending, and program commitments, and justification.

2.4.4.1.6 High-level deliverables

<u>Identify deliverables at both the corporate level and functional level to demonstrate alignment.</u> The review will demonstrate alignment with company goals for financial results, organization structure and processes. So, for example, the Sales VP cannot unilaterally decide to establish an international distributor network organization. While corporate deliverables may define a total sales value, functional deliverables that contribute to the corporate goal will be more specific, such as regional sales targets, or perhaps product line sales targets.

2.4.4.1.7 Contingency and communications plans

Executives will review their high-level plans with the workshop team. These are summaries of those detailed plans developed by the executive with the functional experts who manage the business day-to-day.

2.4.4.1.8   Unresolved issues

Not all issues or opportunities identified will be resolved, during the executive workshop. List items that are not satisfactorily resolved, and include a priority, timetable for resolution, the individual responsible to complete, and the expected goal. The goal may include investment, increased sales, or change in headcount. This summary should be part of the meeting minutes.

Exhibit 21 High Level Activities										
Description	**Notes**	**Priority**	**Resp**	**2016**				**2017**	**2018**	
				Q1	Q2	Q3	Q4			
Data Systems Review		C	J Barnes							
New Product Launch	1	A	G Silva							
Integrate Spain with Corp. Culture		A	G Coreo							

1 - The new products represent a completely new platform for the Company and will represent more than one-third of sales volume within the next 4 years. No expense should be spared.

2.4.5   Identify Integration Issues – Group

Throughout the workshop, executives will present integration plans that explain how they will complete the integration process. Plans will include organization and personnel changes, investments in people, processes and plant, as well as potential write-offs. During the workshop, feedback from other executives may require changes to their proposed plans.

- *Designate an executive to document decisions made, changes to the goals and plans to achieve them, and open items. Document changes for any significant changes to the plans*, such as task name, deliverable description, timeline, costs, resources required, and task dependencies. For example, the Sales VP cannot obtain sales reports until the sales systems are implemented. Conflicts due to prioritization and resource constraints will arise during the integration/transition planning, and should be resolved immediately or listed for follow-up later.

- *The facilitator will review all significant changes to the original plans, and coordinate final updates to the original workshop documents.* This includes the deal summary, the financial summaries, and gap analysis. Revise the transition plan immediately after the meeting - e.g. during the week following the workshop. After updating the operational plans, the facilitator will review the plans to ensure that the most recent financial summaries are reasonable in relation to the operational plans. Finish the update process, including the detailed operational plans, and the updated financials as quickly as possible - e.g. within two weeks of the workshop.

- *If the facilitator believes that the changes made require a formal review, convene a brief workshop to validate the final working plans with the executive team,*

These plans are tentative working plans until the executive team can actually validate all the assumptions and activities once the deal is complete, and the team has access to the acquired Company's personnel and facilities. During the first

101

100 days, validate the plans through discussion with the target Company personnel, observation of actual activities and facilities, and review of documentation to support the assumptions.

2.4.6   Create Detail Plan & Timeline - - Group

Detailed plans and timelines may be created using project planning software such as Microsoft Project or other software developed specifically for M&A transactions. These programs are available either as web-based applications, or for those doing numerous transactions per year, by purchasing the software. Some developers, such as TX2 Systems, have web-based software so that real-time information is available anywhere, anytime around the globe. TX2 Systems (http://tx2systems.com/) is an example of software developed specifically to manage complex M&A transactions. Sample reports from the TX2 System are included as Exhibits 21A-21D. Note that the software follows the normal course of a transaction, and includes information necessary to manage the M&A transaction effectively from inception to complete integration.

ema

Home ▪ All Deals ▪ All Activities ▪ Library ▪ Help

Logged in as Jones | Admin | Preferences | Exit

Sullivan Corporation

| Summary | Team | Synergies | Milestones | Deliverables | Issues | Risks | Assumptions | Notes | Documents | Milestone Map |

◉ Deal Detail

Deal Name:	Sullivan Corporation
Current Phase:	Target
Deal Type:	Acquisition

Code Name:	
Deal Value:	$100M
Target Close Date:	5/12/2006
Business Unit:	Electronic

Web Link:	www.company.com
Business Sponsor:	Ellis, Brianne
Deal Lead:	Christie, Dave

⚡ Major Issues

Description	Owner
Employee retention is 5% below estimates	Christie, Dave
Customer renewals are down 7%	Wood, George

⚡ Major Risks

Description	Owner
Back office migration may be costly because of older SAP platforms being used	Barwell, Graham
Extraordinary conditions could increase the royalty payment.	Aussem, Ed

⚡ Overdue Deliverables

Status	Description	Owner
⬤	Identify and Modify Employees associated to new initiative in Payroll System	Wheeler, Rachel
⬤	How do we make the Plating to Production status happen? (1.0.11.16)	Wood, George
⚡	Determine if the alignment of the quality organization within the company provides adequate focus on independence, and product/process assessment to meet customer needs.	Wood, George

⚡ Assumptions

Description	Owner
Royalty payment schedule will be intergrated into accounting system	Barwell, Graham
New product manager will identify additional product opportunities with revenue potential	Barwell, Graham
The Sales & Marketing team will have detailed Executional Excellence plan ready to be distributed to key executives for approval	Wood, George

File Edit View Favorites Tools Help

ema

Logged in as jmoon | Admin | Preferences | Edit

Home » All Deals » All Activities » Library » Help

Sullivan Corporation

| Summary | Team | Synergies | Milestones | Deliverables | Issues | Risks | Assumptions | Notes | Documents | Milestone Map |

Synergies (hide filter)

Owner All ▾   Synergy Status All ▾   Criticality All ▾   Go

Status ▾	Issues	Description	Criticality	Planned Value	Owner	Functional Team	Edit
●	▶	Distribution Network Expansion	High	$60M	Galland, Violaine	Legal	✎
●		Add-On Product Sales	Medium	$7M	Nevins, Jim	Legal	✎
●		Operating Cost Savings	Medium	$22M	Aussem, Ed	Human Resources	✎
◐	▶	New Product for Existing Product Line	Medium	$1M	Nevins, Jim	Legal	✎
◐		New Market Entry for Product Category	High	$10M	Galland, Violaine	Legal	✎

5 Synergies

Local intranet

Logged in as jhnson1 | Admin | Preferences | Exit

ema

Home ▪ All Deals ▪ All Activities ▪ Library ▪ Help

Sullivan Corporation

| Summary | Team | Synergies | **Milestones** | Deliverables | Issues | Risks | Assumptions | Notes | Documents | Milestone Map |

Milestones (Hide Filter)

Milestone Status All ▼   Functional Team All ▼   Planned Due Date ▼   Owner All ▼   Go

Status	Issues	Description	Criticality	Planned Start Date	Planned Due Date	Owner	Functional Team	Synergy	Edit
●	▼	Create 5-Year Proformas	High	8/22/2006	10/27/2006	Ellis, Brianne	Finance	Synergy: Distribution Network Expansion	✎
●		Identify Leadship Team for New Product Category	Low	8/23/2006	9/29/2006	Wheeler, Rachel	Business Unit	Synergy: Distribution Network Expansion	✎
●		Review Market Opportunity	Low	8/18/2006	2/9/2007	Bechtold, Ginny	Business Development	Synergy: Distribution Network Expansion	✎
●		Review Marketing Strategy White Paper	High	8/18/2006	8/28/2006	Christie, Dave	Business Development	Synergy: Distribution Network Expansion	✎
◐		Finalize Cost Accounting Reports	High	8/22/2006	4/27/2007	Ellis, Brianne	Finance	Synergy: Distribution Network Expansion	✎
●		IT Migration Plan	Low	8/23/2006	2/9/2007	Smith, John	Information Technology	Synergy: Distribution Network Expansion	✎
◐		Review Public Financials	Low	8/18/2006	2/9/2007	Wood, George	Business Development	Synergy: Distribution Network Expansion	✎
◐		Finalize Marketing Plan	High	8/18/2006	3/23/2007	Barwell, Graham	Business Unit	Synergy: Distribution Network Expansion	✎
◐		IT Migration - First 30 Days	High	8/22/2006	4/28/2007	Smith, John	Information	Synergy: Distribution	

Done   Local intranet

105

ema

Logged in as jrosen | Admin | Preferences | Exit

Sullivan Corporation

Summary | Team | Synergies | Milestones | Deliverables | Assumptions | Issues | Risks | Assumptions | Notes | Documents | **Milestone Map**

Milestone Map

Status | Incomplete ∨

	Target	Early Review	Due Diligence	Negotiations	Close	Integration
Business Development	● Review Marketing Strategy White Paper	● Review Market Opportunity ● Review Public Financials	● Valuation Model Review	● Agree on Licensing and Royalty Terms	● Finalize Closing Agenda	● Integration Team Handoff
Business Unit	● Develop Business Case ● Early Alert Process		● Identify Leadship Team for New Product Category ● Develop Marketing Plan		● Finalize Marketing Plan	● Communications Plan - Employees
Finance			● Create 5-Year Proformas ● Run Valuation Models		● Finalize Funding Source	● Finalize Cost Accounting Reports
Legal			● Perform Title Search	● Final Approval of Definitive Agreement		

Local intranet

106

The Executive Workshop will require advance work, which is outlined in the following chart. Note that the work actually begins prior to completing the transaction. The workshop occurs in the first week after deal completion, and additional executive review may be required for significant changes required during the workshop.

Ref	Resp	-4	-3	-2	-1	Closing	1	2	3	4	5	etc.
Exhibit 27												
Mergers & Acquisitions Planning												
Weeks												
2 The Executive Workshop - Framework												
2.1 **Objectives**												
2.1.1 Confirm the keys to valuation												
2.1.2 Review/modify/confirm a high-level business model & financial goals												
2.1.3 Review preliminary organization structure												
2.1.4 Summarize/assess key personnel												
2.1.5 Develop contingency plans												
2.1.6 Develop a communications strategy/plan												
2.2 **Participants**												
2.2.1 Leaders – both sides of the transaction												
2.2.2 Best people essential												
2.2.3 Complete value chain to be represented												
2.3 **Process/agenda**												
2.3.1 Establish Rules of Governance												
2.3.2 Executive Advocates												
2.3.3 Review the Deal												
2.3.4 Review the Operations/Functions – Functional Exec												
2.3.5 Identify Integration Issues – Group												
2.3.6 Create Detail Plan & Timeline - - Group												

107

DAY ONE+

The deal was completed on Monday January 30.

On Tuesday, February 1, in accordance with the plan, the leader of each acquired company read the scripted bullet points, reinforcing that everything would be, "...business as usual...." Several of the business-unit Presidents were local favorites who supported the nearby community - e.g. Pop-Warner football, soccer clubs, the local arts, and regional hospitals. Their charitable work, high-profile contributions, and gregarious personalities raised them to celebrity status. They were ready targets for the local media.

During several of these interviews, these executives mentioned that charitable contributions were decided at the Connecticut headquarters... centralized warehousing ... shifting manufacturing etc. These incomplete statements heightened tensions among the local charities, customers and vendors.

The first round of questions was a follow-up to the initial sound bites. Major customers called and suggested that they would not want to be served from a centralized Connecticut warehouse. Vendors, who relied heavily on each company's local presence, immediately become concerned about losing a major customer. A torrent of emails bombarded the local executives. They immediately forwarded the emails to Connecticut, whose limited staff could only stack the notes for later response.

As the communications' delays continued, local turmoil escalated...

3 Day One

Successful Day One activities establish a framework for the entire transaction. If constituents arrive at the company and cannot get into the building, or do not have proper computer passwords to function, it will be obvious that there is poor planning. Functional executives must develop a master matrix of critical activities, in all functions and locations, including all constituents. Once the matrix is developed, assign the Day One activities. Include all companies in Day One planning, even if some companies will have no changes, since the master matrix will minimize omission errors. One caution - *do not change something on Day One unless it is essential.* Too much change can quickly become chaos.

3.1 Brainstorm critical operating issues

Develop a checklist of all possible activities, which consider all constituents, to identify the activities to complete on Day One. The brainstorming team represents the functional executives and any employees, customers, vendors or other constituents necessary to identify the critical items. During the brainstorming session, identify high impact activities that are critical on the first day.

- *Identify critical constituents to contact on Day One.* The President may want to personally visit or call key customers, vendors or employees with the integration message and plan. The company may also use web-conferences, teleconferences, email, and websites to open a consistent dialogue with the constituents.

- *Items that need Day One attention include:* (Note: These items need not be fully resolved, but the company should communicate with the involved constituents to manage expectations.)

  o Press releases and media packets to explain key elements of the transaction to the constituents.

  o Employee compensation, such as salary, bonus, commissions, health and life insurance, and benefits.

- Outstanding employment offers, current hiring processes, pay raises, promotions, and transfers.

- Security clearances, access to company processes, cash, travel requirements, credit cards, and computer processes.

- Cash management and control activity, loans, advances, and company credit cards.

- Customer pricing, payment terms, contracts, and open purchase orders.

- Vendor pricing, current and negotiated contracts, delivery schedules.

- Government registrations and filings such as Department of Transportation and the Food & Drug Administration.

- Insurance, performance bonds, and licenses.

- Freeze all in-process contracts, employee hiring, expanded outsourcing, and capital spending until the merged company can evaluate how these actions fit within the strategy.

3.2 Review negotiated company purchase, supply and performance contract terms to identify any Day One requirements.

For example, certain executives may be terminated upon deal closure, so it is important to notify the constituents that those individuals are not able to represent the company effective Day One.

3.3 Establish real-time communications processes

- *Establish a clearing-house -e.g. web-accessible for all issues that may affect the success of the transactions. Develop communications processes so that any constituent (inside or outside the company) can raise issues with a designated responsible person, if necessary.*

- *Establish feedback loops so that constituents who identify issues receive prompt feedback.*

Ensure that executives and other management personnel know contact information - e.g. by function and location. Executives and managers should actively listen and observe for Day One integration issues. Tactics can include:

o   Management-by-Walking-Around;

o   Phones, teleconferences, Webinars;

o   E-Mail;

o   Blogs, which may require close supervision depending on the tone of the transaction.

3.4   Conduct integration team meetings to discuss/resolve issues.

Coordinate Day One activities well in advance of the event. If possible, include the Target Company employees and executives in the planning process prior to Day One. Despite thorough transition planning, errors and oversights will occur. If you have a process to record, manage and resolve issues, the integration will succeed.

In the value chain, support functions perform services for the primary functions. Include representatives from these functions on all other functional teams, since they will respond to Day One issues. For example, the Information Technology group should implement a plan to establish passwords, security control, and access to critical systems such as fringe benefits.

- *Implement a real-time communication process so that errors and oversights are immediately communicated to the correct level for fast resolution.* Resolve all issues as quickly as possible, even if it is a temporary solution.

Example Matrices follow:

	Exhibit 28 Constituents											
	Employees			Customers			Vendors			Other		
	Day 1	Week 1	Month 1	Day 1	Week 1	Month 1	Day 1	Week 1	Month 1	Day 1	Week 1	Month 1
Logistics												
Freight - company receiving Parts stocking Freight broker	Consider all the activities and interactions completed with these groups. Think about the impact of the transaction, and mark when it might be appropriate to communicate with these individuals.											
Operations Manufacturing floor supervisors Technicians Engineering												

- _List all functions on the vertical axis, and identify constituents across horizontal axis._ The matrix should represent all functions, activities, and constituents affected in any company involved in the transaction. While it seems to be a daunting task, a 1-2 hour meeting with the constituents/representatives will identify all the major items requiring attention. Not everything need be resolved immediately, but any actions that require immediate attention will be addressed.

3.5   Day-One Execution

The ideal Day One has little major change, but rather is one of open communications discussing the transaction, and the philosophy of the combined company. Do not change anything on Day One that is not essential. However essential items, such as updating a license to operate a fleet of trucks, must be completed on time, or the Company may not be able to serve its constituents.

Execution will be the key to Day One success. Organize the integration teams to anticipate problems immediately at the opening of business. *Establish clear communications lines so that constituents understand how to raise questions - e.g. personally, by phone, E-mail, blog etc. Implement a tracking system to identify trends as transition issues arise.* In addition to providing an immediate response to questions from constituents, schedule a brief daily transition team meeting for the first week to identify and resolve issues. Team members should be proactive and prepare summaries of issues and trends to manage the environment, and not just react to individual issues.

The following plan shows that most of the work for Day One must be completed prior to the transaction closing, since Day

One (Closing), each of these items must be implemented.

Exhibit 29												
Mergers & Acquisitions Planning												
				Weeks								
Ref	Resp	-4	-3	-2	-1	Closing	1	2	3	4	5	etc.
3 Day One												
3.1 People												
3.1.1 Employees compensation & benefits												
3.1.2 Employment offers/promotions												
3.1.3 Freeze other personnel decisions until organization review completed												
3.1.4 Establish lines of communication & business processes for action - e.g. approvals levels												
3.1.5 Meet/communicate with key customers & vendors discussing the acquisition- use prepared script												
3.1.6 Establish communications with other key constituents - e.g. regulatory agencies etc.												
3.2 Processes												
3.2.1 Cash management process established & fully implemented.												
3.2.2 Ensure that all payroll process & benefits procedures are in place.												
3.2.3 Establish updated security measures (access to websites, email, cash etc.)												
3.2.4 Establish rules of governance - e.g. approvals levels, personnel actions, reporting relationships etc.												
3.2.5 Establish/confirm business process with key customers & vendors.												

Etc.

LATER THAT MONTH - THE FIRST 100-DAYS

The Company survived Day One+.

Although the first few weeks the Company executives were in react mode due to emergency activities (setting up regional bank relationships; completing many registrations; reacting to major customer & vendor requests; resolving numerous regional executive leadership challenges; establishing rules of governance for the many new regional executives; etc.) the COO and CFO were finally ready to pursue the First 100 Days objectives. One of the first

117

objectives was to interview the leadership team of each acquisition to establish a working relationship and define the rules of governance. Surprisingly, some of those entrepreneurs who eagerly sold the business were now somewhat reluctant to perform as employees, rather than entrepreneurs. Several of the leaders would be a challenge to manage from Connecticut, and some of them simply refused to cooperate - almost as if they weren't acquired. Disillusioned former owners now met informally to discuss issues with the PE owners. Scheduled routine communications were often cancelled due to the number of emergencies - ranging from key employee turnover, to frequent systems failures.

Before the acquisition, most of the acquired companies were managed based on the owner's in-depth knowledge of the business. Few - if any - performance metrics were available, since the owners intimate knowledge of the entire business was sufficient to manage. The initial corporate reporting requirement was, "... business as usual ..." Unfortunately, some of the companies closed the monthly financials within 20+- days - some only closed quarterly to satisfy bank requirements. Financial statements were basic - high-level P&L and Balance Sheet. Since the owner and leadership team at each location were so familiar with the business additional formal reporting was unnecessary.

As the COO and CFO toured the companies, met with the functional leaders of these acquired businesses, and assessed their capabilities to perform as Corporate functional executives, they discovered that many of those leaders were not yet capable to serve as national functional leaders. Worse yet, they were already working 50-60 hours a week, just to keep business at the status quo. Business growth was elusive. The Company would need to hire outside experts to bridge the immediate talent gap, and also spend tens-of-thousands of dollars to train the execs for the larger national role. The spending was not budgeted.

One of the keys to profit growth - establishing a national logistics platform with coordinated regional warehouses - would be impossible for at least one year. The data systems that were initially considered adequate for the national network were crash-prone and out of maintenance by at least 2 years. The system simply would not work as the national logistics driver. This $500k investment to upgrade the system wasn't forecast in any transitional plan.

The manufacturing operations at two of the acquired companies had complimentary product lines that would be ideal for national distribution. The acquisition plan also included launching new products that the Company expected to produce within 90-120 days, raising factory utilization to nearly 70%. Profits increases due exclusively to leveraging the factory utilization were forecasted to total nearly $1 million during the first 12 months. Unfortunately engineering support in the California operation, running at 55% utilization, was minimal. The Company could either:

- *Hire an engineer to support the operation, with a 5 month delay and an unplanned $125k initial profit impact, or*
- *Engage a contract engineer at a monthly cost of nearly $30k*

- *Temporarily relocate an internal engineer to raise California productivity. This would reduce effectiveness of the transferring unit, and cost an additional $14 per month travel cost.*

These costs were not included in any forecast.

Due to the lack of engineers, anticipated new product launches would be delayed. First year impact would total about $500k.

During the tour of the manufacturing facilities, in these first few months, one of the plant managers presented a list of equipment needs to the COO. The cost of previously postponed maintenance, and essential replacement equipment tallied to $750k. He also mentioned that the existing equipment and minor upgrades would not be capable of producing the planned new products. When asked why he didn't mention this before, he said, "No one asked."

4 First 100 Days

Exhibit 21 depicts the operational activity and deliverables required to be successful in any transaction. There are three major operational elements of the transaction:

- Day One activities and deliverables

- The First 100 days of activities and deliverables

- The Second 100 days of activities and deliverables

Exhibit 30

Day One	First 100 Days		Second 100 Days	
Analyze & Execute	Analysis & Strategy	Detail Design, Build & Execute	Sustain & Harvest Benefits	Synergy
A s s e s s & P l a n	· Understand keys to value · Assess hi-level business model · Review organization & structure · Review comp & bonus/ fringe · Review processes & systems · Prepare hi-level gap analysis · Prioritize activities	· Design process flows · Define tech & facilities · ID & train personnel · Relentless execution Understand keys to value	· '100' day status check · Reassess priorities · Align activities to priorities	· '200' day status check · Strategic assessment

...Deliverables ...

Day One	First 100 Days		Second 100 Days	
E x e c u t e	· Organization & structure · Comp & bonus plans; fringe · Personnel alignment · Prioritized processes & systems · Implementation timetable · Financial assessment · Contingency plans · Communications strategy	· Detail project plan · Procedures developed · Personnel trained · Active project management & reporting · Processes implemented · Communications strategy execution · Contingency planning	· Detailed status review · Priority assessment · Financial assessment · Updated project plan	· Strategic assessment

122

The First 100 Days will include the integration team's validation of all the assumptions, plans and expected results developed in the executive workshop. It will also include a rapid execution of those near-term plans, which will be the foundation of a successful integration. Executives will now have open access to the constituents who may have been unavailable prior to the closing and can now review all the assumptions and plans developed previously without their insight. Identify broad strategies and deliverables in the workshop to establish the magnitude and pace for the integration process. Once the high-level strategy is acceptable to the M&A leadership team, finalize more detailed planning using the functional resources that will actually complete the work. For example, it would be a waste of time to plan an engineering Bill of Materials process on a new SAP data system, if the company changes strategy to use an Oracle system.

During the First 100 days, constituents should meet frequently to validate, assess, plan and begin execution of plans to merge the entities. Meetings should take place on a scheduled basis. Short cycle tasks such as cash management controls may take place daily, while a function's overall review meeting may take place weekly. Executive management attention is critical during the first days after the merger to assure the constituents of the merger's importance, and to listen and respond to issues that surface. Decisiveness is essential.

Throughout the First 100 days, the Executive Transition Team should meet at least weekly to monitor performance versus objectives, and to modify goals based on real world information. The transition executives will prepare formal and informal communications for all constituents, including vendors, customers, employees, and agencies. Constituents recognize that the First 100 days will be disruptive and require more work than usual. Extra staff, overtime, frequently changing short-term priorities are the norm. Know that your competitors are anxious to take your best employees and customers during this period, and adjust your actions to avoid such losses.

4.1   Analyze & Develop Strategies

Thus far in the transition, the *"To Be"* state has been defined, the executives have assessed the *"As Is"* status of the companies affected by the transition, and high-level plans have been developed and approved by the executive team. Once the deal is closed, implement the following actions immediately:

> o   Execute the "Day One" activities identified in earlier meetings to avoid business disruption in any function, in any location affected by the transition. Validate "Day One" activities

with the target company constituents before the close to avoid business disruption.

o Within the first ten days after closing, the transition team leadership will coordinate high priority activities to _validate the key valuation assumptions, high level plans and strategies, organization structure, policies and costs developed and approved in the Executive Workshop._ The leadership will have direct access to the target company personnel, vendors, and customers, possibly for the first time. Conduct a mini-workshop with key personnel so that they can begin the detail planning.

o Within the first ten days after close, company employees will develop detail transition plans, including people, processes and plant, to achieve the defined acquisition goals. Detail planning should include accountabilities, costs and required resources, timing and coordination among all the companies and functions involved in the deal. Prioritize the plans based on company benefit, cost and resources available, for the overall master plan approved at the Executive Workshop. In an ideal M&A transaction, complete the planning before the closing to accelerate the integration process.

o Execute the detail plans and communicate - outbound and inbound. Carefully manage the environment, which includes employees, customers, vendors, other constituents, since the environment may now differ significantly from pre-deal. At each major transition plan milestone, notify the transition team of any significant variance from plan to be sure that other areas that may be affected can modify their plans.

o After the First 100 days, reassess the transition strategy and status versus the acquisition plans.

4.1.1 Understand Keys to Valuation

See Section 2.1.2 for the summary of the keys to valuation. *Coordinate a mini-workshop meeting with the integration team members to review the transaction summary and the keys to valuation, so they can align their activities to achieve the goals.* Validate the assumptions related to the high-level summary so that all team members have a common understanding of the goals and interim objectives. Review any significant variances with the integration team leaders immediately to determine whether the strategy should be adjusted.

4.1.2   Assess Hi-level Business Model

See Section 2.1.1 Review *the approved high-level business model (as confidentiality permits) with all the team members, and validate the assumptions developed at the Executive Workshop so that the teams can align their activities to the approved strategy.*

4.1.3   Review Organization Structure

Based on the high-level business model approved at the Executive Workshop, develop *detailed organization charts, identify actions and develop job descriptions, and complete training within the first few weeks of deal closing. Include constituents, from any organization involved in the transaction.* For example, new systems and operating procedures may require training for vendors and customers to use a new website effectively. Assess the span of control, the number of layers in the organizations, use of contractors and temporary employees and confirm the *""To Be"* organization.

4.1.4 Assess Personnel

Evaluate the constituents to understand current and future capabilities, and their fit within the "To Be" organization. Identify and develop retention plans for key employees and constituents, including those both inside and outside the company who are essential to the successful merger. *Develop transition plans to align the organization with the approved organization. Evaluate personnel performance and the required performance in the "To Be" state, and identify any gap to reach the "To Be" status.* Determine if the gap is due to inexperience, poor training, or capability, and develop a plan to train, reassign or terminate employees not expected to meet future requirements. Identify the specific actions required for every employee throughout the organization(s) within the first 30 days.

Develop a plan to transition redundant employees and other constituents. Treat employees with dignity and respect, pay fair termination settlements and retraining costs, and provide job search support. As you complete these transitions, know that your competitors, customers, vendors and local communities will evaluate your actions as a guide to your normal business methods.

4.1.5 Review compensation and bonus; fringe **benefits**

Evaluate the elements of constituent's compensation (inside and outside the company). Develop the expected "To Be" state and timeline, and a transition plan to achieve the goal. There are three steps in the compensation review:

- o *Document and evaluate the "As Is" structure at the companies, and include every form of compensation and benefits to any constituent (include vendors, government agencies, active and retired employees, temporary and contract employees).* Compensation and benefits include salary/wages, bonus, stock options and grants, perquisites (auto allowance, tuition reimbursement etc.), life, health and dental insurance, 401K etc. *Follow the money* to avoid missing a compensation element. For example, outside contractors may not be included on organization charts.

o *Evaluate compensation such as union representation and contract status, expected negotiation timeframe, employee contracts, vendor contracts, and terms and conditions for all other payments.*

o *Finalize the "To Be" state details* based on the assessments, and compare to those approved at the Executive Workshop. Document major variances and review the variances with the transition team leaders.

o *Once a final "To Be" state has been accepted, define action plans to reach the "To Be" state,* which includes expense and capital, as well as other critical information, such as headcount, and organization structure changes.

4.1.6 Review Processes/Systems

Evaluate all systems and processes, including outsourced systems such as FedEx, logistics, in all companies involved in the transaction to determine if transition plans are required. Validate the systems and processes identified in the Executive Workshop, as well as all other systems and processes that were not considered in the Workshop. List and assess the quality of the processes used in each location, and their potential use in the "To Be" combined company. The *"To Be"* performance should meet an established standard. The summary will identify duplicate or questionable processes that may be eliminated, or optimized if moved to other locations. As multiple locations are identified in the master matrix, assess the process quality and scalability.

Reviewers should always seek a better method to complete the task, and not just assume that one of the existing methods is the best. Since the companies are involved in major process and systems changes, consider upgrading all the systems instead of just patching existing systems together. For example, each company may have outdated

CRM processes, and the best solution is to upgrade to a new system. See Exhibit 20 for an example of a process summary. This type of summary should be prepared - on a priority basis - for every significant location, and for every significant activity performed in the merged company.

4.1.7 Validate Hi-Level Gap Analysis

Validate the Executive Workshop process gap analysis. Also, identify any processes that require improvement, based on a more thorough review, and summarize the key elements of change required. Summarize essential information that describes the issue, expected resolution and timing, the potential benefit, and costs, and identify whether the costs are capital or expense. These summary pages should be logged and monitored at periodic meetings. The gaps will be identified by comparing the *"As Is"* status with the *"To Be"* state.

Exhibit 31				
Technology Gap Assessment				
		Year		
		1	2	3
Issue Number:	Revenue:			
Resolution:				
Responsibility				
Description of Resolution:	Expense:			
	Capital:			

Prepare a gap analysis (the difference between the *"To Be"* organization, technology, plant) and the *"As Is"* operations. The gap analysis will describe the issue and the proposed solution. The gap analysis also will describe the costs and expected benefits to evaluate in the context of the overall integration process.

4.1.8   Prioritize Activities

Prioritize activities based on the acquisition objectives and resources available. An integration project will have major priorities managed at the senior level, and lesser priorities within the functional areas. For example, the president may personally meet with every major customer in the First 100 days, while the sales manager may update the customer data base files within the First 100 days. Quite often, the plans will require constituents to complete activities during the first few weeks of the integration. Since plans are seldom executed exactly as expected, changes in priorities may be required. Based on the governance rules established for approved activity changes, revise the priorities to achieve the integration goals using current information rather than an outdated plan. Review these gap summaries with the Executive Transition team at periodic meetings.

4.2 Analysis & strategy – Deliverables

Review the detailed strategy. A thorough review may not take place until after the closing, since the acquirer may not have access to the target company's records, staff, and plans. During the Due Diligence and negotiation phase of any transaction, high-level analysis and strategy will be developed to estimate the amount of investment, including expense and capital, resources, and approximate timelines for implementation, as a basis for negotiation and valuation. Since the plans are at a high level and somewhat imprecise, these broad plans are often not executable at a department level.

Expand the plans to reflect specific resource allocation, deliverables, priorities and timelines to meet the strategic goals, and manage these plans in a traditional project management process. For example, it may be clear at a high level that the company needs a new $1 million engineering design data system, and the system implementation will require 5 months of effort. However, a detailed implementation plan including work force project loading, specific activities, and specific capital and expense spending will be required to execute the plan.

Major changes from plans identified during the Executive Workshop should be reviewed at the Executive level to ensure alignment within the organization. If significant changes are made to spending levels, the transaction may not meet established objectives.

4.2.1 Organization structure

Design the detail organization structure that best fits the expected "To Be" state outlined in the valuation process, without regard to the existing organizations or personnel, such as unions, and existing locations. Detail design includes specific job titles and responsibilities, and reporting structure. When the overall design is completed and approved by the integration team leadership, assess the existing structure, personnel, and process to develop a detail plan to move from present to future. The structure should reflect the *"To Be"* state span of control, number of layers, management philosophy (centralized, or decentralized), and culture.

4.2.2 Organization Culture

Validate the organization's culture in all locations, with the understanding that cultures may vary by location or function. Identify inconsistent cultures in high priority areas as an unusual culture may disrupt integration plans. Identify the *"To Be"* culture, and develop plans to migrate to the *"To Be"* state. For example, some cultures are very formal, rigid, and well organized. If such a company acquired an informally managed entrepreneurial company, by design, the culture of

137

the acquired company may never change, since their value is based on their entrepreneurial spirit and creativity.

Culture is a major variable in a successful merger, and culture change is one of the most difficult activities to complete. If there are major culture differences, detailed plans to explain the culture goals as well as the path to achieve the goals are essential. Validate the initial observations from Due Diligence (see Exhibit 6) once you have access to all personnel and all locations.

4.2.3   Compensation, Bonus and Fringe Benefits

4.2.3.1   Compensation and Bonus Plan

Assess compensation and bonus plans for all companies involved; develop the "To Be" state, and create a bridge plan to achieve the "To Be" state. Thoroughly analyze all elements of the compensation at the companies. Ideally, complete the analysis before the merger is finalized so that announcements discussing the compensation plan can be made upon deal closure. Compensation includes salary, wages, bonus, stock options, stock grants, 401-k, pension, deferred compensation plans. Realign performance driven

138

programs as soon as practical to avoid conflicting priorities. Also, since the integration will require exceptional work and effort, develop a program to compensate the team properly for delivering a successful merger. Compensation programs are extremely personal and should be immediately addressed. If compensation and benefits are not properly assessed and changed to motivate, the constituents will not effectively support the transition.

4.2.3.2   Fringe Benefits

Fringe benefits include all non-cash benefits to any constituents, including both formal and informal programs. Benefits can include, but are not limited to, vacations, sick time, personal days, tuition reimbursement, birthday recognition, and special performance awards. Discuss the programs with the acquired company executives to determine the best course of action.

4.2.4   Personnel alignment

Prepare organization charts, job descriptions, approval's authorities (capital and expense spending, hiring and firing, and contract approvals levels), and span of control.

Personnel alignment will directly affect the organization's performance. As strategic and near-term goals are developed, align the organization to the company goals. Document and distribute the goals to affected employees. Prepare a master summary that describes the overall organization, and key elements of the alignment. Integrate compensation, such as incentives, bonuses, and recognition programs, with organizational goals throughout the structure to reinforce alignment.

4.2.5   Processes & systems

Develop a matrix of all processes and systems for any acquired organization and the base organization. Identify every activity in any organization to determine actions required:

- o   List and document all activities for every function.
- o   *Assess the quality* of the activity to determine if the activity meets the requirements. Determine if remediation is required for those not meeting standard, and estimate the resources, such as personnel, expense, and/or capital, required,

estimate time to complete, and benefit to the organization. If similar activities are performed in all locations, always select the best activity for future use, or plan to upgrade the activity to the "To Be" state required.

- o *Prioritize the activities based on costs and benefits*, and coordinate with other functional areas and locations to get the best results more quickly.

- o *Plan resources to meet the priorities established.* Use external resources if adequate resources are not available in-house. It is often far more expensive to miss priorities than to invest initially.

4.2.6 Implementation timetable

Establish detailed implementation schedules, but also ensure that the senior executive team reviews suitable macro-project timelines periodically. Establish critical milestones and report progress against these objectives on predetermined schedules such as at the weekly executive meeting. Each time the high-level implementation timetable is reviewed by the integration team leader, confirm with the executive team that activity objectives are on track, or review remedial actions to bring the project back on schedule.

4.2.7 Financial assessment

Assess the established acquisition objectives and reconfirm that all significant issues have been identified and resolved. Each executive should confirm that the financial aspects of the project are on schedule or explain remedial action to achieve the goals. Complete this step after the entire organization has reviewed people/constituents, processes, and plant/assets to understand the "As Is" and the "To Be" state, the gaps between the two states, and the organization has created detailed plans to move to the "To Be" state. Include a financial summary of any significant changes from plan. This should include timing, since inefficiencies during integration are potentially significant, and the impact on constituents, such as customers, vendors, and employees, may be significant.

4.2.8 Contingency Plans

Develop contingency plans that allow the combined organization to meet the established merger goals. Discuss contingency plans at each formal review. Determine if the plans need modification at each meeting, and/or begin contingency plan execution if the integration project is not meeting objectives. Each element of the contingency plan should have an executive sponsor who owns the responsibility for execution.

4.2.9 Communications strategy

Review the communication's strategy, and reconfirm the key elements of the strategy with the new company executives. Consider all the constituents, both inside and outside all the companies, timing and frequency of communications, media that can be used and the probable audience response. Media may include newsletters, e-mail, web posting to the company website, personal town hall meetings, and small group meetings with the constituents. For example, if a company discontinues operations at an acquired business location, the employees at that location will be affected. However, all company employees could be concerned about their continued employment, since employee seniority or specialized skills may affect employees throughout the company. Anticipate the constituent reaction and plan accordingly.

4.3 Detail Design/Build/ implement – Activities

Earlier in the M&A process, high-level plans were created to integrate the companies. The design/build/implement segment of the First 100 days will focus on execution. Management will design processes, train personnel, and develop systems as described in detail plans developed by the integration teams. Execution describes specific activities, timelines, assigned personnel, costs and so forth, for the entire integration project, including all departments, functions, locations, and personnel. This may affect both companies, as each functional executive who attended the Executive Workshop and their staffs will implement the plan to achieve the *"To Be"* state. Complete these activities throughout the organization, and involve all constituents - employees, vendors, customers, agents, and agencies.

In addition to completing the tasks, *the team will prepare and review with management periodic project status reports. The integration teams will conduct formal project review meetings throughout the organization, as you would do with any major*

project, to ensure that the detail activities are being

completed as required. Meeting frequency and content will

depend on the task priority and complexity. Conduct

department or function meetings, daily or weekly - -

depending on the nature of the tasks. For example, cash

management procedures should be resolved immediately so

daily meetings may be appropriate. However, changing

paper stock, logos, and selected printed material may be

managed weekly.

The definition of assets includes any asset used by the

company, whether they are tangible or intangible; owned,

leased, or borrowed.

4.3.1   Design Process Flows

The merger goal is to combine companies or selected

functions into an organization that provides more profit to the

overall organization. Each company often has a complete

value chain, resulting in duplicate functions or processes

within the functions. Process flows must be modified or

eliminated to reach the merger goals. As process flows are

modified, people and systems need change or replacement,

retraining/programming. Each element of change requires time and investment. It also entails risk. The integration team is responsible for understanding the "To Be" state, the "As Is" state. They must define the change required, and then manage the risk so that the change is properly implemented. Design process flows for all processes requiring modification, and prioritize the flows based on greatest value to the organization. The process flows will describe the business processes that will be in effect when the *"To Be"* state is achieved. Identify all the steps necessary to move from the current status to the "To Be" status.

4.3.2   Technical systems and facilities identified

Inventory and document all technical systems and facilities in both organizations, and include in process items on order/under contract. This summary should provide a level of detail that allows the executive to assess the required changes to reach the *"To Be"* state. For example, systems documentation should include summaries of hardware and software used in the day-to-day function, as well as those systems in development. The summaries will describe the status of technical assets and facilities, and include items such as unlicensed software, or facilities not in usable condition and might require extensive repair or replacement. The summary will identify additional investments required to have a fully functional technical structure and facilities when the *"To Be"* state is finally achieved.

At the conclusion of the review, the integration executives will formally confirm that the expected *"To Be"* state can be achieved, with a summary of resources, expenses/capital, and timeline necessary to reach that level.

4.3.3   Develop Procedures

The integration team and all participants throughout the organization will review every function, every activity, and every procedure and identify and change procedures necessary to achieve the "To Be" state. Procedures should be thoroughly documented and complete whereby the standard of performance, defined within the scope of the "To Be" business model, can be achieved.

4.3.4   ID/Train Personnel

As procedures and facilities/assets have been modified, *select and staff the redesigned processes with appropriate personnel, and train them to meet the required "To Be" state of performance.*

4.3.5 Execution

Ruthlessly execute the implementation plans. Develop and achieve aggressive execution plans since delays in execution will disrupt the entire constituency. The best employees, customers and vendors etc. may leave the merged company and go to the competition. During integration periods, good competitors understand the confusion and inefficiency and lure the best from the merged companies.

The hidden cost of Inefficiency during the integration process can be as much as 50 percent, and only the after-affects will be observed in lower profits, lost customers, employees and vendors. Effective project management during the initial 100 days is critical and will include formal and informal reporting and performance measurement.

4.4 Detail Design/Build/Execute – Deliverables

The First 100 days establish the performance expectations for the entire integration process. _Develop and maintain open candid communication channels throughout the entire constituency._ Sub-groups within the merging companies may have their own agendas, their own cultures, and business drivers. During the First 100 days, team members should continually assess the environment, modify plans as necessary, and flawlessly execute. Prioritize deliverables to provide the most benefit to the merged companies, and identify dependencies that can affect the entire project. For example, if a company does not properly develop new system specifications, systems cannot be designed and implemented. _If deliverables are delayed, understand the impact on the integration project and assign resources accordingly._

4.4.1 Detail project plan

Prepare a master detailed project integration plan, which includes all significant steps, costs, and resource requirements that are based on a thorough understanding of the project interdependencies. Manage the plan using progress reports in progressively more detail as you proceed

149

down through the organization. Schedule progress report meetings based on level within the organization, the critical nature of the tasks, and the impact on the company as a whole.

4.4.2 Develop Procedures

Modify activities and related procedures as organization responsibilities change. *Prepare and document detailed procedures to reflect the changed activities.* Procedures should include a statement of purpose, required resources, contacts and activities to be performed, estimated time to complete, skill levels and advance training required, and a description of the ultimate deliverable. Develop procedures consistent with the integration priorities and accelerate those that add the most value first.

4.4.3 Train Personnel

Train all personnel as to the purpose, all the required steps to complete a task, and the basic skills to perform the task (both hard and soft skills). Consider training in groups so that personnel are cross-trained on essential processes, and train in advance of going live to ensure that there are fewer missteps. Maintain up-to-date training processes to reflect the current procedures.

4.4.4   Active project management & reporting

Aggressively manage the First 100 days based on the established priorities. During the first week of the transition, conduct daily update meetings to resolve new issues, and resolve open issues from earlier tasks. After the initial weeks of activity, executive meetings can be weekly. Use judgment to determine the meeting content and frequency, but concentrating on *exceptions to the schedule will* yield the best results in the least time. Discuss only significant activities that are off schedule, or significant new issues. The meetings should be action oriented, decisive, and brief. Prepare minutes and schedule follow-up sessions. At the conclusion of each meeting, each executive participant should be able to state that either the project is on schedule, or the listed actions are in place to bring the project back to the required timeline.

4.4.5   Processes implemented

Implement the integration processes as scheduled in the prioritization. *Monitor the process changes to ensure that the desired result occurs - progress toward the "To Be" state. Modify processes if they do not achieve the desired goal, and modify the written procedures and training to reflect any changes.* The business world, competition, and constituencies change frequently and may often require changes to the plan. Maintain open communications throughout the organization, and be flexible to a changing the schedule.

4.4.6 Communications strategy execution

Review the communication strategy that outlines long-term objectives and the short-term tactics outlined at the Executive workshop. It is essential that both outward and inward communication processes be established. *Establish "help" lines for reporting problems, and issues, establish and publish e-mail addresses to receive feedback from inside and outside the company. Consider establishing blogs that provide an uncensored communication process, since feedback is essential to a successful integration process.*

Plan these communications so the participants can achieve their goals on schedule and enjoy the feeling of success. Provide routine updates to the constituents to inform them of accomplishments, and subsequent merger steps. Updates may be provided through the following:

- Weekly newsletter (e-mail or web posting) with overall integration/transition progress.

- Periodic town hall meetings

- Periodic live or recorded web casts, which may also be available on an integration website for later viewing.

4.4.7 Contingency planning

At the Executive workshop, executives prepared contingency plans that may offset major unfavorable events. Unfavorable events, such as product introduction delays, increased competition during the transition period, or lost key employees or customers can affect sales, profits, cash flow, plant/assets, systems and processes. Contingency planning identifies those potential unfavorable events, and creates alternative plans that will offset the unfavorable impact.

During the First 100 days, validate the contingency plans,

and begin to execute those that are required.

			Exhibit 32 Mergers & Acquisitions Planning											
							Weeks							
Ref		Resp	-4	-3	-2	-1	Closing	1	2	3	4	5	etc.	

4 First 100 Days
  4.1 **Analysis & Strategy - - activities**
    4.1.1 Understand Keys to Valuation
    4.1.2 Assess Hi-level Business Model
    4.1.3 Review Organization Structure
    4.1.4 Assess Personnel
    4.1.5 Review Comp & bonus
    4.1.6 Review Processes/Systems
    4.1.7 Prepare Hi-Level Gap Analysis
    4.1.8 Prioritize Activities
  4.2 **Analysis & strategy – Deliverables**
    4.2.1 Organization structure
    4.2.2 Organization Culture
    4.2.3 Comp & bonus plan
    4.2.4 Personnel alignment
    4.2.5 Prioritized processes & systems
    4.2.6 Hi-level implementation timetable
    4.2.7 Financial assessment
    4.2.8 Contingency Plans
    4.2.9 Communications strategy
    4.2.10 Detail Design/Build/ Execute - - Activities
    4.2.11 Design Process Flows
    4.2.12 Tech/Facilities Defined
    4.2.13 Develop Procedures
    4.2.14 ID/Train Personnel
    4.2.15 Execution
  4.3 **Detail Design/Build/ Execute - - Deliverables**
    4.3.1 Detail project plan
    4.3.2 Procedures developed
    4.3.3 Personnel trained
    4.3.4 Active project management & reporting
    4.3.5 Processes implemented
    4.3.6 Communications strategy execution
    4.3.7 Contingency planning

SECOND 100-DAYS

During the first 100-days, 8 key people left the acquired companies, and needed to be replaced immediately. Costs incremental to the transition plan now tabulated to about $3 million of expenses for temporary labor, interim executives, training, search fees & relocation, T&E - all to be incurred during the first year.

Additional capital expenditures totaled nearly $2 million for new data and telecom systems, manufacturing equipment and building and office fixtures.

Product launches have been delayed by at least 12 months, and the overall centralized warehousing and logistics plans were scrapped due to customer requirements. The only customer concessions obtained were to concentrate "C" class items in two regional warehouses - East Coast and West Coast. This would delay order fulfillment by 48 hours.

5 Second 100 Days

During the Second 100 days, longer-term projects will continue to be implemented. Project management skills will focus on the routine changes in those items that are less visible, but still essential to the successful transition. Constituents who are working on these projects will require positive reinforcement since the initial impact of the merger is gone. Invite constituents who are meeting their objectives to periodic executive meetings to present their results, gain exposure, and feel a sense of accomplishment. Congratulate them on their performance.

During the Second hundred days, <u>begin to harvest the improvements planned. Document the value created, and broadcast the success</u>. The Second 100 Days is a chance to reassess and realign expectations and tasks to be completed. The meeting format should be similar to the first Executive Workshop, but with considerably more insight into the processes, risks and opportunities.

Exhibit 23 highlights the major activities and deliverables for the Second 100 Days.

Exhibit 33

	First 100 Days		Second 100 Days	
Day One — Analyze & Execute	Analysis & Strategy	Detail Design, Build & Execute	Sustain & Harvest Benefits	Synergy
Analyze & Execute Plan	· Understand keys to value · Assess hi-level business model · Review organization & structure · Review comp & bonus/fringe · Review processes & systems · Prepare hi-level gap analysis · Prioritize activities	· Design process flows · Define tech & facilities · ID & train personnel · Relentless execution. Understand keys to value	· 100 day status check · Reassess priorities · Align activities to priorities	· '200' day status check · Strategic assessment
Execute ...Deliverables...	· Organization & structure · Comp & bonus plans; fringe · Personnel alignment · Prioritized processes & systems · Implementation timetable · Financial assessment · Contingency plans · Communications strategy	· Detail project plan · Procedures developed · Personnel trained · Active project management & reporting · Processes implemented · Communications strategy execution · Contingency planning	· Detailed status review · Priority assessment · Financial assessment · Updated project plan	· Strategic assessment

157

5.1 Second 100 days – Activities

At the beginning of the Second 100 days, *coordinate a one-day Executive Workshop to reassess the progress of the First 100 days.* Transition executives will report their progress against the established objectives and discuss the next 100 days goals and activities.

5.2 Sustain & Harvest Benefits

Compare benefits and major accomplishments achieved to plan, and explain major variances. Include financial results for items originally planned during the First 100 days, such as reduction of Days Sales Outstanding (DSO) in accounts receivable by 5 percent or $2 million.

5.2.1   100 Day Status Check

Coordinate the Executive workshop to understand the existing "As Is" situation, the planned "To Be" goal, and the status of scheduled major projects. All the value chain elements and the constituents will be included in the status check. Effectively, update the presentations used in the first Executive Workshop to reflect the knowledge gained, and revised goals and objectives. Once again, executives will discuss their assessments of the integration, and the "To Be" state. The "To Be" state and the activities that will be used to achieve the objectives may be somewhat modified from the initial workshop. Review all the activities to ensure a coordinated effort, and common goals among the executives.

5.2.2   Reassess Priorities

Reassess priorities with the newly gained knowledge from the First 100 days of observation and activities completed. Expect changes to established priorities, since the earlier workshop did not include complete insight into the target organization. Unfortunately, change may be required since not all the initial objectives established during the First 100 days may have been completed.

5.2.3 Align Activities to priorities

As necessary, adjust the priorities to reflect the knowledge gained from the First 100 day's results. Priorities may shift during the meeting, as other executives' goals may require adjustment for the company benefit, such as delayed installation of data systems, or spending beyond budget. Adapt priorities to new facts arising during the integration.

5.3 Second 100 days – Deliverables

Once the priorities are established, align the activities to the priorities, and *develop/reconfirm specific deliverables for the next 100 days.* The project plan will include names, dates and specific deliverables so that the activities are coordinated within the company. The project plans will have enough detail so that daily, weekly and monthly meetings can measure performance against the objectives.

5.3.1 Updated project plan

Once the transition executives have updated the detailed plans, the workshop will again familiarize the entire team with the expected activities and deliverables, and will allow overall coordination among the functions.

6-MONTH REVIEW

The COO and CFO met at the local pub for several hours to discuss the first 6 months activity.

Later that night, the COO sent an email to the CFO. His message - entirely in the subject line -

"We need to plan and execute to a much finer degree if we ever have the courage to do this again."

6 Synergy

At the conclusion of the second hundred days, reflect on the progress achieved and identify the benefits realized thus far. Synergies planned are often not realized, and the end of the second hundred days is an ideal time to reassess the acquisition in total. In addition to planning an abbreviated workshop to understand the integration status when compared to the plan, this is an ideal time to reevaluate the acquisition strategy and synergies realized.

7 About the Author

Mike Gendron is the founding partner of CFO Insight LLC. He has extensive global experience throughout Europe, Latin America and the Far East in companies ranging in size from "Business Week's Hottest Growth Companies in America" to billion dollar global organizations. Industry experience includes high-tech electronics, telecom equipment, FDA regulated operations, and industrial instruments.

During his career, he has been the CFO of global corporations - both public & private - and he has extensive executive experience in Fortune 500 corporations. He has led or participated in M&A buy/sell transactions in France, Germany, China, Mexico, Canada and the US in industries such as high-tech electronics, telecom equipment, FDA regulated and industrial instruments companies.

He frequently speaks and writes about topics such as mergers & acquisitions, strategy, and E-Business, and he maintains a website (http://www.cfoinsight.net) dedicated to financial management, and mergers & acquisitions.

In addition to flying high-performance airplanes as an instrument rated pilot, Mike enjoys backpacking, skiing and golf. Mike is Vice-Chairman of the Management & Entrepreneurship Advisory Board at Xavier University, and a member of numerous private company advisory boards.

Other Books by Michael P. Gendron

- "Cashing Out @ Full Value: A Novel-Guide for 'Boomers' Selling the Family Business" (2014 - Company Cues)
- "Doing the M&A Deal: A Quick Access Field Manual & Guide" (2007 - Company Cues)
- "Creating the New E-Business Company" (2006 - Southwest Publishing)
- "Integrating Newly Merged Organizations" (2004 - Praeger Publishers)
- "A Practical Approach to International Operations" (1988 - Greenwood Press, Inc.)